Informed Leadership

David Ribott

PASSIONPRENEUR® PUBLISHING

'Working with David has been one of the most powerful growth experiences of my leadership journey. His ability to create space for honest, deep reflection—while always bringing it back to practical action—is a rare gift. David's coaching style is genuine, grounded, and entirely focused on helping you evolve—not just as a leader, but as a person.

'His book, *Informed Leadership*, captures that same spirit. It challenges leaders to go beyond surface-level fixes and instead strengthen their mindset, their intent, and their impact. The focus on Presence, Purpose, and Practice is a simple yet transformative framework. It reminds us that leadership isn't about control or constant motion—it's about showing up with intention, aligning to what matters, and committing to getting better every day.

'David's work challenges you to lead with more awareness and integrity, and I'm grateful for the impact it's had on my own journey.'

—Fahed Ghanim, CEO, *Majid Al Futtaim Lifestyle*

Informed Leadership is a deeply grounded guide to becoming the kind of leader people actually want to follow. David Ribott offers a clear, actionable roadmap for navigating complexity with purpose, clarity, and integrity.'

—Dorie Clark, executive education faculty at Columbia Business School and *Wall Street Journal* bestselling author of *The Long Game*

'David's wealth of experience from his days as an athlete to helping transform companies across MENA have been distilled in this book that starts with informed leadership but ends with impact.'

—Diana Wu David, CEO of Future Proof Lab and ranked #2 Global Futurist by Global Gurus

'David is credible and experienced. If you are looking for someone to challenge you as a leader, and your assumptions, I think his book will encourage a deeper, reflective conversation with yourself.'
—Dustin Seale, Regional Managing Partner EMEA, Heidrick Consulting and co-author of *Lead Through Anything*

'*Informed Leadership* is a clear-sighted and deeply practical guide for leaders navigating complexity. David combines grounded experience with a values-based framework that invites us to lead with greater awareness, resilience, and intention. This book doesn't offer easy answers—but it does offer the right questions, and a model that equips leaders to make better choices, even in uncertainty. A must-read for any senior leader committed to personal growth and organizational impact.'
—Dr. Hannah Haikal, Senior HR Leader Business and one of ASIA'S 100 WOMEN POWER LEADERS for 2023

'*Informed Leadership* spoke directly to the real-life challenges I face as a leader. It seamlessly blends professional insights with coaching wisdom, encouraging deeper reflection on your leadership position and purpose. It equips you with the clarity and confidence to lead with intention and navigate complexity. A must-read for anyone who wants to lead not just effectively, but meaningfully.'
—ALJohara ALMandil, Head of Digital Innovation Lab, Jeel

'*Informed Leadership* is both a call to courage and a compass for clarity in today's complex world. As a senior leader in education in the Middle East, I found David's insights deeply resonant and practical. Grounded in first principles—Respect, Integrity, Dignity, and Empathy—Ribott's ABCs of leadership offer more than a model; they provide a moral and operational guide. His work challenges leaders to confront blind spots, lead with alignment, and embrace discomfort with purpose. This book reminds us that leadership excellence is intentional—and that real change begins with personal responsibility and self-awareness.'

— **Kenneth D. Grcich, Ed.D., Associate Dean for Student Affairs, Georgetown University in Qatar**

'*Informed Leadership* is a rare blend of clarity, strategy, and practical wisdom. By grounding leadership in first principles, the book strips away complexity and reorients the reader toward what truly matters: purpose, alignment, and performance to deliver long-term prosperity. It challenged me to rethink how I lead—not just in terms of decisions and outcomes, but in how I align teams and drive meaningful impact. This is a must-read for leaders who are serious about building sustainable, purpose-driven organizations.'

—**Sandy Damm, Multi-time CEO and author of**
SME GLOBALISATION: How to Maximize Your Company Value in a Cost-Efficient Way

'As a people leader in a global strategy consulting firm, I see firsthand the urgency of leadership, that is both principled and pragmatic. *Informed Leadership* delivers just that—a framework grounded in empathy, accountability and bold decision-making. David captures the real-world challenges leaders face, from conflict avoidance to performance inflation, and offers actionable insights to drive meaningful cultural and organizational transformation. This book is a great read for any leader committed to evolving themselves while building teams that can thrive in complexity.'

—Isabell Stobwasser, Executive Director of Talent IMEA, Oliver Wyman

'*Informed Leadership* is a sharp and pragmatic guide for senior leaders navigating today's complex business environments. David brings a rare blend of strategic insight, real-world experience, and practical frameworks that resonate well with readers. His use of analogies, combined with a clear focus on purpose, performance, and accountability, makes the content both engaging and actionable. The RIDE mindset and ABC leadership traits are particularly useful and straightforward to apply. This book is a valuable resource for any leader serious about growth, impact, and building a resilient, high-performing culture.'

—Damian Ellacott, Acting CEO, NEOM Airlines

Informed Leadership

Applying first principles to unify purpose,
heighten performance,
and maximize prosperity

David Ribott

PASSIONPRENEUR®
PUBLISHING

Print: 978-1-76124-230-4
E-book: 978-1-76124-232-8
Hardback: 978-1-76124-231-1

Publishing information
Publishing and design facilitated by
Passionpreneur Publishing
A division of Passionpreneur Organization Pty Ltd
ABN: 48640637529

Melbourne, VIC | Australia
www.passionpreneurpublishing.com

Dedication

For my son Leo Matias Ribott, whose curiosity and energy reminds me every day of a famous Walt Disney saying: 'If you can dream it, you can do it.'

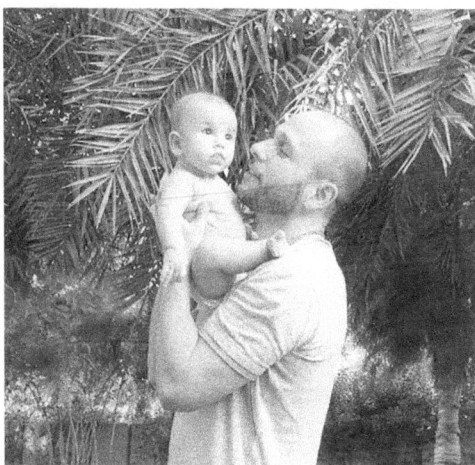

This photo always reminds me of what's important in life, and makes my heart smile every time I look at it. Daddy loves you buddy!

Contents

Introduction

Let me first say that a leader's job is an unenviable position. Yes, the salary of a C-suite executive can be high. It is nice to have the title. It is also nice to have a corner office and to work on one of the higher, more exclusive floors in the building. But it is a lonely job, it is extremely difficult, and there is very little sympathy for leaders.

Plus, as the rate of change has become exponential, the demands on senior leaders seem to increase faster than they can develop themselves. It can feel like you are merely treading water, with no real solution in sight.

I have come across leaders in organizations who are content to tread water, who are checked out and/or ambivalent about their responsibilities and duty to the organization and the people on the teams they lead. I assume, since you are reading this, that you are not one of them.

You want to be a purposeful and successful leader. You are committed to developing your skills and abilities. Yet such are the demands placed on you that you may not even notice you are treading water, and your commitment to development often goes unnoticed.

Besides, some of the challenges you face fall outside your locus of control. There is little you can do about the state of the marketplace or global events, for example. The solution is to look inward and work on yourself, since you *are* within your locus of control.

You might think this is unrealistic, or even idealistic, especially if your organization resembles a battlefield full of metaphorical landmines where taking the wrong step could lead to catastrophe. Staying in shape is hard with a full-time job— even harder if you are a leader with a demanding remit. But if you want a decent quality of life, there is no getting around the need to eat healthily and go to the gym and align your lifestyle with what you want for yourself. Being a purposeful leader within an organization, if that is your intention, is no different.

Yes, it will be hard to overcome these challenges, but it is possible to do so. It is not enough, as a leader, merely to 'tick boxes'. Best practice and best outcome are not the same, and only leaders who have endured real trials and tribulations can discern the difference. If you are able to access that level of awareness, you will be less attached to the challenging situations themselves, less vulnerable to the triggers that have previously tripped you up, and better able to navigate a way forward.

I often get asked, 'What problems do you solve for your clients?'. In simple terms, I clean up messes and make things right during times of extreme challenge and complexity by helping organizations to battle-test strategy and cultivate effective leaders. How do I do that? My clients tell me that I skillfully balance business strategy and leadership coaching conversations while helping them read the political landscape so that they can navigate it with integrity.

I am a board and leadership advisor who has worked with some of the most respected leaders in the MENA region—as well as some who poorly reflected the tenets of business ethics (one of whom is currently serving time in prison for defrauding their organization). With experience as both an executive and a non-executive, I am able to connect the dots for the leaders and organizations I work with because I understand their world and the pressures and challenges they face. I know what it is like to get through an M&A because I have participated in some of the biggest banking M&As in the region. I know what it is like to prepare an organization for an IPO because I have previously supported a utilities sector client in what was a landmark IPO for the region.

My ability to be tactful in approaching sensitive topics helps clients digest strong but necessary feedback—necessary because sometimes there is no getting around having to tell a senior leader, 'You cast a big shadow, and that's making it difficult for your team to operate effectively and meet the needs of the business.'

My experience shows that most organizational problems center on the impact an absence of accountability has on organizational culture and the business's bottom line. The famous saying, 'What you permit, you promote. What you allow, you encourage. What you condone, you own.' is truer than many realize. When, in my conversations with committed senior leaders, they come to this realization—i.e. that their inaction has contributed to the state of things just as much as negligent leaders' bad behavior—they suddenly see the way forward, that transformation is possible.

Even if you aren't regularly posting on social media or merely passively viewing content, I am sure you will be aware of the vast volume of posts and comments on leaders who merely manage, on what makes a business culture toxic, on all the things that are wrong with organizations. What these online critics generally lack, however, is skin in the game. They are not leaders themselves; they are spectators viewing from the sidelines, so their ideas lack the kind of impact needed to create momentum for transformation.

I wrote *Informed Leadership* because I *do* have skin in the game. And from my conversations with clients, I saw a trend emerging in terms of what works and what doesn't work in organizations. I saw certain themes recurring, which led me to develop a model for leaders to follow. Over the years, I fine-tuned and battle-tested it to make sure it held up in real-life situations. It does, and the final version—the Informed Leadership Model—is set out in the following pages.

The model is based on the four pillars of informed leadership: Respect, Integrity, Dignity, and Empathy, which enable leaders to operate on a solid foundation. That operation in turn requires four qualities, the ABCs of informed leadership: being Anti-fragile, Bold, Clear, and Deliberate. With that foundation and those qualities, a leader will be in a position to focus on the three Ps of success: Purpose, Performance, and Prosperity.

Informed Leadership is not meant to knock you or make you feel bad about yourself as a leader, but rather to point out some of the common leadership pitfalls and suggest ways in which you might avoid them, encourage you to step outside your comfort zone, and place yourself and your leadership on solid ground.

It will show you how to adopt an informed approach to leadership by building and strengthening your leadership mindset and qualities, so that you will be better positioned to focus on the needs of your organization for it to achieve success.

Informed Leadership is about being in a position to make conscious choices about what we are doing, rather than more or less haphazardly going along with things and therefore being at the mercy of whatever situation arises—like a boat adrift in the ocean that is driven one way and then the other by the wind and the waves. Being able to make better choices gives us more control over our business outcomes.

If we are to overcome the challenges that cause interference in our organizations, to transform their culture, and to lead them successfully, we must commit to informed leadership.

The role of leaders is not easy, and even a commitment to self-development is no guarantee of success. Everyone make mistakes, and no one is perfect. But as informed leaders, we will be tolerant of those mistakes and see them as an unavoidable part of our progress—not as obstacles or roadblocks, but as the way forward.

PART ONE

The Need For Informed Leadership

Many leaders today—across almost all industries, regardless of the size of their organization and whether it is publicly listed, privately held, government backed, or itself a government entity—haven't had the training they need to lead the people and the departments they find themselves heading. In many cases, they are not conscious of or informed about best practices or ways in which to do things more efficiently and optimize for success. They have often been promoted on the basis of their technical skills or of previous successes, but previous success isn't always an indicator of future success. So when a leader takes on a new role or there is a change in their remit, there is often a gap between their competencies and the needs of the role—and, given the increasing pace of change in today's business world, they have little time to catch up. Instead, as their remit continues to evolve over time, that gap only widens.

In this first part of the book we look at the blind spots leaders most commonly experience in managing their relationship with their direct reports—and at the causes and consequences of those blind spots—before exploring a different way of approaching that relationship based on first principles and an understanding of human nature.

1

Leadership Blind spots

Being a leader at any level in an organization is difficult. Most organizations are too big for every feature to be controlled and all outcomes factored in. The more senior you are, the more influence you have, but that doesn't necessarily mean that you have an easier time of it. You still have your battles to fight and you still need the skillset to be able to be effective as a leader. Having worked as an advisor with countless leaders in difficult situations, I have empathy for you. I understand your challenges.

At the same time, it has to be recognized that confidence in leaders is today at an all-time low. According to Russell Reynolds Associates' Leadership Confidence Index,[1] only 62.5% of senior managers had confidence in their leaders in the first

---

1   Russell Reynolds, *Leadership Confidence Index*, https://www.russellreynolds.com/en/insights/reports-surveys/leadership-confidence-index (accessed March 25, 2025).

half of 2024—a figure that had declined from 67.5% just three years previously. This lack of confidence is measured in terms of executive capability, executive team behavior, and how the executive team tackles critical issues.

In working with senior leaders over the years, it has become clear to me that this lack of confidence can be traced back to certain blind spots that leaders are susceptible to, certain situations in which leaders commonly 'drop the ball'. It is these that I want to dive into in this chapter.

In occupational psychology terms, competency models and factor analyses show that two of the most difficult competencies for leaders to develop are conflict management and talent development.[2] As such, these are highly predictive indicators of future success—or failure. We therefore begin this investigation of leadership blind spots with an exploration of the reasons why these two key competencies are so problematic, coupled with an assessment of the potential consequences of a lack of competence in these areas.

Conflict management

Arguably, the more challenging of the two is conflict management; and, while I have extensive expertise in the field of mediation, I am under no illusion that building the skill of conflict management is easy.

Conflict is unavoidable. We have ideas, which create conflict. We make plans, which run into conflict. We engage with people,

2   e.g. Korn Ferry, *Korn Ferry Leadership Architect™ Global Competency Framework*, https://store.kornferry.com/en/product/5d7bc4a3-c28a-47eb-b8d1-47bc293e65ff (accessed March 25, 2025); Korn Ferry, KFLA Technical Manual, https://www.scribd.com/document/354060738/KFLA-Technical-Manual (accessed March 25, 2025).

which causes conflict ... In any organization with between one and a thousand employees, it is certain that there are going to be moments at which conflict arises.

In any organization with between one and a thousand employees, it is certain that there are going to be moments at which conflict arises.

I would go so far as to say that the relationship between employer and employee is inherently antagonistic; at least, it is commonly regarded as such. Employers often don't trust their employees and vice versa. We know from our experience of the Covid pandemic, for example, that remote work *works*; yet many employers are now insisting that their employees come back to the office—a move that is inevitably regarded as a way of monitoring them, as a sign of an 'unhealthy' relationship.

It requires a high degree of emotional and social intelligence, first to navigate the causes of conflict and then to drive results through other people while leveraging that conflict for the potential of innovation and creativity. Without the necessary skills, conflict management becomes a matter of trial and error, a hit-and-miss affair with unpredictable outcomes.

Worse, there is a tendency for leaders to develop a strategy of conflict avoidance that amounts to ineffectual compromise. In their mind the leader may be thinking, 'This is what's best for the business,' when in fact they are only dealing with the symptoms instead of getting to the heart of the issue at hand. And when you deal only with symptoms, prevention is not addressed. When preventative measures are not anchored, there will simply be a repeat of the same cycle of problems.

There is a tendency for leaders to develop a strategy of conflict avoidance that amounts to ineffectual compromise.

Only a handful of industries are good at managing conflict, and they usually have specialists (mediators, ombudsmen, and others) whose role is to carry out this type of work. Without their training, most leaders struggle to manage conflict effectively—or at all.

In his 1965 paper 'Developmental Sequence in Small Groups,'[3] psychologist Bruce Tuckman identified four essential stages in group development: forming, storming, norming, and performing—later adding a fifth, mourning or adjourning. It is during the second stage, storming, that conflict arises in the form of disagreements and personality clashes, which must be resolved before the group can progress to the next stage, norming. Yet this crucial stage is often skipped, leaving that conflict unresolved and hampering further development.

The problem comes from regarding conflict as inherently negative. If we do so and either resign ourselves to it or simply ignore it and hope it goes away, we abdicate our responsibility as leaders to repair and recover situations that have gone sideways.

Decision paralysis

Poor conflict management leads inevitably to another blind spot that organizations commonly have, which is decision paralysis—the inability to take decisions in a timely manner (or even at all). I can't tell you how many clients I have worked with where an important decision, such as whether to allow employees to work remotely or not, comes up and the relevant

---

3   Bruce Tuckman, "Developmental Sequence in Small Groups," *Psychological Bulletin* 63, no. 6 (1965): 384–399. https://psycnet.apa.org/doiLanding?doi=10.1037%2Fh0022100

leader's response is simply to put their head in the sand and pretend the problem isn't there, hoping that by the time they pull their head out again, it will have magically resolved itself.

Decision paralysis isn't merely a sign of weakness; it is often a defensive mechanism. Again, in my role as an advisor, I have seen countless people who have summoned up the courage to take a decision but have then been shot down or publicly shamed when that decision turned out to be ill-advised—with the inevitable consequence that they become gun-shy about making important decisions, simply kicking the can down the road until a decision doesn't need to be made or is made by someone else.

Decision paralysis isn't merely a sign of weakness; it is often a defensive mechanism.

Another challenge we encounter if we are conflict avoidant or haven't really worked on our ability to manage conflict is that we lose sight of the potential benefits of conflict and how to turn it to our advantage—which we will be looking at in the next chapter.

Talent development

The other particularly difficult competency for leaders to acquire is talent development, simply because if we aren't properly trained, we don't actually know what good performance looks like. We are all too easily seduced by the *appearance* of what good is, and there is often a halo effect whereby, if somebody has a friendly disposition and a pleasant personality and is easy to work with, we believe they are good at their job. When you start to dive into the way that they go about their work or line-manage their teams, however, you can often find that they are actually ineffective, inefficient, or even chaotic.

Talent development requires an understanding of how human performance works, how to motivate people, how to assess where people are in terms of the business's needs, and how to devise appropriate development strategies, followed by the capacity to monitor performance systematically over time.

When I worked in various industries and organizations, I would often hear line managers say, 'That's HR's job' when it came to developing a team member's skills. But HR is usually too far removed from that particular employee's day-to-day output and performance to be in a position to manage or develop them, whereas their line manager is far better placed to do so, because they are closer to them and 'see their work day in and day out.'

The challenge is to have the right set of lenses to be able to focus on what good should look like, see how people can be moved from what they are currently doing what is expected of them, and progressively close that gap. Often, employees are themselves unclear on what constitutes good performance. They might seek guidance from their line manager but, depending on the latter's level of emotional intelligence and ability to communicate, that could be either a fruitful conversation or a frustrating one.

Often, leaders will simply say, 'Go out there and get it done,' which may be inspirational to some extent, but is unhelpful in that it lacks the hard metrics to clarify what the target is in measurable terms, therefore creating more chaos than confidence.

If our direct reports are to be effective and successful, they need to know what success looks like.

If our direct reports are to be effective and successful, they need to know what success looks like.

When I work with senior leaders and look at how they performance-rate their teams, I am often shocked at how many 5s and 4s are given—on a scale of 1 to 5, where 3 means 'meets expectations', 4 'exceeds expectations', and 5 relates to performance that is off the scale, while 2 indicates 'underperformance' and 1 signals that performance is catastrophic. I ask them, 'Where are the 1s and 2s? Because if you aren't happy with the way your team is performing, I would expect to see a lot of 1s and 2s.' But when I see that everyone is at a minimum of 3, meaning that they 'meet expectations', and that people are receiving a 4 when they are just doing their job, it is clear that there is 'performance inflation': something is wrong with the leaders' evaluation approach.

So I ask them, 'Okay, what justifies a 5?'. And I look at their performance metrics, and I discover that what justifies a 5 to one leader and what justifies a 5 to another is quite different. It is perhaps understandable that there might be some variance between departments that are active in very different ways, such as commercial, HR, facilities management, and marketing, but if that is the case, it becomes very difficult to manage any kind of cross-functional team. However, there is often a glaring absence of consistency in terms of what 'good' looks like, even within the same department. If we aren't consistent in our expectations, we won't be managing the same level of performance. And if we aren't managing the same level of performance, we're going to get inadequate performance.

One way in which performance is inconsistently rated derives from a common confusion between good, effective work and 'hard work'. If someone is always working late and on weekends, they are generally considered to be a 'hard worker' and consequently given a 4 or a 5; whereas someone who leaves the office at 5 o'clock every afternoon and never takes work home is thought to be doing no more than is absolutely necessary and therefore given a 3. But it could be that the person who works late and on weekends is actually *under-performing*: They are having to do extra hours because they are inefficient and don't know how to manage their workload.

In fact, research shows that a law of diminishing returns applies to long work hours: The longer we work, the more our performance and productivity fall off.[4]

The tendency to overrate employees is another symptom of conflict avoidance. Leaders are often failing to give employees the regular feedback they need to help them identify what they are doing well and what they are not doing well, and know how to change the way they are carrying out their work so that they can meet the needs of the organization or their team.

The tendency to overrate employees is a symptom of conflict avoidance.

When I dig into what leaders are doing to support a direct report to whom they have given a performance rating of 2, the answer is all too often 'very little'; and that person will be shocked by the feedback because they have had no indication from their line managers that they weren't doing well the entire year.

Allowing 'adequate' performance to pass for 'good' performance, on the other hand, is another abdication of our responsibility as leaders. There is an old saying that 'What we permit is what we promote.' In other words, we are simply perpetuating bad habits and the status quo, where people are

---

4   See, e.g., Erin Reid, "Why Some Men Pretend to Work 80-Hour Weeks", April 29, 2015, https://hbr.org/2015/04/why-some-men-pretend-to-work-80-hour-weeks (accessed March 25, 2025); Pencavel, J., *Diminishing Returns at Work: The Consequence of Long Working Hours* (Oxford University Press, 2018).

just coming to work and going through the motions until it is time for them to go back home.

As we will see in Part 2, one of the ways in which a CEO can neglect their responsibility is not giving enough clear feedback to their direct reports on what their expectations are or not being available for conversations with direct reports. This means that there is no clear roadmap showing them what success looks like, so a lot of the time they are left having to guess.

If as leaders we are to set up our direct reports for success, we need to communicate clearly what our expectations are.

When I visit a new client's site and I carry out a diagnostic of the way people are working and the way leaders are operating their teams, I often come away wondering, 'Why do they tolerate that?'. Leaders are in a position where they can impact the way work works, where they can develop their people so that it works better, and yet they often fail to do so.

Worse, if what is expected in terms of performance isn't clearly communicated downstream to an employee, this can lead to disengagement. According to an April 2024 Gallup workplace survey,[5] only 30% of US employees are 'actively engaged' in their work and there is a downward trend in engagement, where employees feel increasingly detached from their employers, have less role clarity, and experience lower satisfaction with their organization and less connection to its

---

5   Jim Harter, "U.S. Engagement Hits 11-Year Low," *Gallup Workplace*, April
     10, 2024, https://www.gallup.com/workplace/643286/engagement-
     hits-11-year-low.aspx#:~:text=Last%20year%2C%20Gallup%20
     found%20U.S.%20employees%20were%20increasingly,to%20
     feel%20someone%20at%20work%20cares%20about%20them
     (accessed March 25, 2025).

mission or purpose. Another recent poll by the Pew Research Center[6] among workers who quit their jobs revealed that well over half did so because they felt that they had no opportunities for advancement and that they were disrespected at work. A similar survey by Statista[7] gave 'lack of career development/ advancement' as the top reason and 'uncaring/uninspiring leaders' as the third most common reason for employees quitting jobs between April 2021 and April 2022.

Such statistics highlight the fragility of the relationship between line managers and their direct reports and make it clear that the absence of conflict management and talent development are key contributors to the breakdown of that relationship and lack of success as a leader.

The implications of conflict management and talent development being difficult to develop as competencies for leaders don't end there. It has a knock-on effect on the whole spectrum of a leader's role and the problems an organization can encounter in its day-to-day operations. Through my experience of working with clients I have come to realize that all of an organization's problems, no matter what industry it is in, come down to a lack of focus on what I call the three Ps: purpose, performance, and prosperity, resulting in a misalignment of purpose, inadequate performance, and the absence of prosperity.

---

6   Kim Parker and Juliana Horowitz, "Majority of Workers Who Quit a Job in 2021 Cite Low Pay, No Opportunities for Advancement, Feeling Disrespected," *Pew Research Center*, March 9, 2022, https://www. pewresearch.org/short-reads/2022/03/09/majority-of-workers-who-quit-a-job-in-2021-cite-low-pay-no-opportunities-for-advancement-feeling-disrespected/#:~:text=A%20new%20Pew%20Research%20Center%20 survey%20finds%20that,reasons%20why%20Americans%20quit%20 their%20jobs%20last%20year (accessed March 25, 2025).

7   Martin Armstrong, "Why People are Quitting Their Jobs," *Statistica*, July 25, 2022, https://www.statista.com/chart/27830/reasons-for-quitting-previous-job (accessed March 25, 2025).

We will look at each of these problems now—and will be returning to the three Ps in Part 3, where we will see how misalignment of purpose, inadequate performance, and the absence of prosperity can be transformed into aligned purpose, heightened performance, and maximized prosperity by applying the principles set out in Part 2 of this book.

Misalignment of purpose

When the ability to manage conflict and to develop talent is low, or absent altogether, it is going to become extremely difficult for a leader to stay aligned with the organization's purpose, as expressed in its mission statement, because they themselves are not grounded enough in themselves and connected enough to what the organization represents in the marketplace to be able to take on and cascade that purpose and to operationalize it in their day-to-day work.

When this is the case, we end up with 'mission creep'—i.e. deviation from the stated purpose of the organization—where leaders behave and act in a way that may be the very antithesis of that purpose and direct reports begin to ask, 'Why are we doing this? This goes against our mission statement.'

No matter what area you sit in in the hierarchy of your organization as a leader, if you aren't able to embed and embody the purpose of your organization and then operationalize it within your work stream, your department, or your team, they are going to have a hard time understanding what it looks like. They will lack the direction they need and feel not only that they are 'not going anywhere' (in terms of talent development and job progression), but even that they don't know where they are supposed to be going.

Without that clarity it also becomes more 'costly' (in terms of time and efficiency) for them to do their job, especially if they have multiple functions or are working in cross-functional teams, since they waste time and effort trying to figure out what they should be doing.

Absence of accountability

Accountability is another difficult thing to develop, but as leaders we require it in order to be able to move our part of the business forward on behalf of the wider organizational needs. But when we are not grounded to a purpose, whether personally or as an organization, our North Star—our guiding light—is not clear and it is much more difficult for us to understand what is acceptable and what is not acceptable. This then shows up in the way we hold accountability.

If a leader is inconsistent with what they deem to be acceptable, they will have inconsistent performance standards and therefore inconsistent quality of delivery. If there is unequal treatment of people on a team by a particular line manager as a result, that is also going to sour the team dynamics and the workplace culture. Rifts will show up between people on a team because, if Person A feels that they are working hard and that Person B is not working as hard but is also not being held accountable for that, it is likely to have an impact on Person A's motivation to do a good job. Again, it is a question of 'What we permit is what we promote.'

If a leader is inconsistent with what they deem to be acceptable, they will have inconsistent performance standards and therefore inconsistent quality of delivery.

When there is no discipline around giving feedback, when there is a lack of due diligence in terms of performance and an absence of quality in terms of output, you are not going to end up with an organization where excellence is the culture; you are going to end up with a fragmented workplace culture, where some people are working harder than others, where some people are being held accountable and some people are not.

Downstream within your organization, people will then simply revert to survival mode. After all, most of them won't have the kind of financial independence that would allow them to leave the organization without having another job in place. They probably have a family with children to bring up or elderly parents to care for, which are always going to be their primary considerations, whatever difficulties they might be having digesting their managers' approach to accountability. So they will simply think, 'Why bother? If our line manager is happy with Person B's performance, I might as well just keep my head down, not put my hand up, not say anything at meetings for fear of being shot down or publicly shamed, and keep my mouth shut so it doesn't look like I'm just being disagreeable.'

Where, then, is the creativity and innovational spark that your organization needs to stay competitive in the marketplace if this is the attitude that is permitted and then unconsciously promoted? Are we simply creating a culture of learned helplessness and stifling our organization's ability to change and transform?

And if enough people put their heads down or decide to check out at work, disengagement becomes the default setting, as the data suggest. And once that happens, you, as their leader, don't even notice that there is anything wrong, because everyone around you is behaving in the same manner—including your own leaders. So why should you stand out by trying to apply higher ethical standards?

If enough people put their heads down or decide to check out at work, disengagement becomes the default setting.

As we shall see, if there is no culture of accountability, there will also be inadequate performance, because the prevailing disengagement of employees will mean that they are not performing as effectively and efficiently as they could or should be—and, incidentally, often having to stay longer at work to complete their basic duties.

Politics at work

When there is misalignment of purpose, 'politics' can quickly become a problem. Politics arise when individual leaders or individuals cluster together and try to carry out their own agendas, their own 'missions'. And politics can show up at all levels of an organization.

I was once asked to support an organization that was reaching maturity and thinking of restructuring. I began by carrying out an internal audit of its current performance; the first thing I noticed was that there was a serious lack of quality in certain areas. I explained this to the senior team and we set about devising a program to improve performance in those areas. We saw straight away, however, that there were people who were resistant to the changes we were proposing—not because our program was inefficient, but rather because they disagreed with the premise that their level of performance wasn't to the standard that the organization expected. From the very start, clusters of people were banding together behind the scenes to sabotage the program.

Inadequate performance

Politics at work also hurts the collective output of the organization. If clusters of people are playing politics at work, if self-interest and individual agendas are taking priority over organizational needs, what is that going to do to the performance of the organization? If people are working against the collective, no matter what high horse they think they are on or how they try to rationalize it, they are working against the organization and against the purpose for which the organization exists.

Toxic work culture

The more we permit politics and bad behavior at work, due to an absence of accountability, the more they are going to grow. The more they are given a license to grow, the more toxic they will become. And once you have a toxic workplace culture, everything becomes much more difficult. Because there is resistance everywhere, there is no single clear path to any outcome. Every aspect of everyone's job becomes more laborious, stressful, and time-consuming.

---

*The more we permit politics and bad behavior at work,
due to an absence of accountability, the more they
are going to grow.*

Everything we do at work requires cross-functionality at some point. No work is done in isolation; the higher-stakes the initiative, the more cross-functionality is needed. But if there is no alignment on what a collaborative effort should look like, any joint project becomes drawn out. Anything that requires any kind of agreement or consensus or layering in terms of, 'This team does this part, and that team does that part' leads to conflict and delays. And delays have an impact on budget, which affects productivity ...

In a toxic workplace culture, even the best people will eventually get worn down. If they have been forced by the absence of accountability to adopt 'acceptable' behaviors just to survive and have continued to plow through them despite their dissatisfaction with them, they are very likely to burn out—while those who are content to just 'go with the flow' are likely to stagnate because, 'Why put more effort in if I am already getting a 5?'.

As the name suggests, a toxic environment also has a negative impact on people's self-esteem. No one wants to be unproductive at work; it is not a great feeling. When you leave work, what do you have to feel good about? What are you proud of? And how do you feel on a Monday morning when it is time to go back to work?

Silo mentality

If this is your existence, it is very easy to retreat into your own 'silo'—which may be your team or your vertical—and, instead of collaborating with other teams and other departments, accuse them of being the problem. 'It's finance's fault that we can't get things done. They're always putting obstacles in the way,' or 'It's compliance's fault. They're always stifling our ability to be commercially agile.' As we will discuss in Chapter 6, no one is always right and no one is always wrong, but it is highly unlikely that anything is 100% someone else's fault. With a silo mentality, however, we can convince ourselves that a failing is entirely another team's fault or another vertical's fault or another department's fault.

No one is always right and no one is always wrong, but it is highly unlikely that anything is 100% someone else's fault.

In retreating into our silo, we are also protecting ourselves. There is comfort in spending time around people who share the same groupthink. But the truth is, the longer we stay in that mentality—the longer it is permitted and promoted—the more downtrodden, depressed, and defeatist we become.

Absence of prosperity

Misalignment of purpose and inadequate performance have a knock-on effect on prosperity. By prosperity I mean the level of investment by the organization in its workforce—in other words, the social contract between them.

In the 1950s and 1960s, and even as late as the mid-1970s, many people worked for a single organization throughout their career, and they were loyal to it because their employer was loyal to them. And at the end of their 30 or 40 years' service, they retired with a gold watch and a pension. That social contract no longer exists, and employees today rarely stay with the same organization for more than five or 10 years, which means that what we have is a very muddled understanding of the employer–employee relationship and unclear expectations on both sides of the equation: those of employees toward their organization and those of organizations toward their employees.

From the employees' point of view, why should they commit to an organization that might decide, to reduce its workforce (call it 'optimization' or 'right-sizing' or what you will) and terminate their employment? From the organization's viewpoint, why invest in an employee if they are likely, from one moment to the next, to jump ship and go work for a competitor?

For a leader today, the question is therefore: Under these circumstances, how do I achieve business continuity and remain competitive? To do so, I must attract the best people. Without talent, we can have no competitive edge. But if there is an absence of accountability and our organizational culture is toxic, why would those people want to work for us? If we don't get the purpose and performance right, we are not going to get prosperity right.

If we don't get the purpose right and we don't get the performance right, we are not going to get prosperity right.

If we don't get that interaction right, there is going to be a constant shift in competitiveness and productivity at organizations, whether we like it or not. We can accept the status quo as 'inevitable', or we can change it and create a vision of something fruitful at the end of the tunnel. To do so, we must confront what is happening and allow ourselves to be better informed so that we can take better decisions on how we want to lead at work.

This is the subject of our next chapter.

Summary

Being a leader at any level in an organization is far from easy, but certain blind spots are common to many leaders, principally how to manage conflict and how to develop talent among their workforce. Because both skills are challenging, leaders tend to avoid conflict and miss potential. These failings can lead to decision paralysis and a lack of accountability, which will result in mission creep, disengagement, a silo mentality, and a toxic work culture. Together, these factors cause inadequate performance and an absence of prosperity.

We have to get the relationship between line manager and direct report right in order to set up both people for success. We need to ask: Are we equipping them with the skills and resources that they need so that they can transfer these to the people they are line managing in the departments that they are leading?

2
Seeing The Way

In Chapter 1 we looked at two of the most difficult competencies for leaders to develop, conflict management and talent development, and I asserted that doing so requires a foundation of intellectual and emotional maturity. So how do we get there?

The process starts with awareness, which is essential to improving our understanding of the difficulties inherent in leadership and of the ways in which we can resolve them.

Awareness

While senior leadership is meant to be looking at long-term financial sustainability, being faced with a succession of problems to solve they are more than likely to be tempted to take shortcuts, to achieve quick wins and short-term success.

The trouble is, short-term success doesn't always translate into long-term success because the parameters are often quite different; what looks like success in the short term might not meet the conditions for success over the long term.

The first step in this process, therefore, is awareness: opening our eyes to everything that is happening within our organization—and especially to things that are simply tolerated, that we permit and thereby implicitly promote.

Coming into organizations from the outside, I am often amazed and baffled by the amount of stuff that is tolerated, when a relatively simple course correction could steer the organization out of an impasse or through a storm. As an outsider, I can often see the problems clearly, but when you are inside the machine, it can be really difficult to make out what is going wrong and why, never mind what needs to be done to fix it. As leaders, we often cannot see the forest from the trees: We are so distracted by day-to-day problems that we fail to pay attention to their underlying causes.

When you are inside the machine, it can be really difficult to make out what is going wrong and why, never mind what needs to be done to fix it.

We also need to open our minds to the possibility that the way we are doing things is not the best way, that there may be other ways that will lead to better outcomes. Key to this increase in awareness is a change in our attitudes toward conflict and accountability.

Conflict as a positive

Conflict is a part of life. It is unavoidable. In saying that, I am not suggesting that we should have active conflict in our lives, but that we need to become comfortable with conflict by understanding the conditions that create it. We should not be afraid of what conflict represents, but realize that within conflict lies an opportunity for growth.

We should not be afraid of what conflict represents, but realize that within conflict lies an opportunity for growth.

A lot of the time, conflict is accidental. For example, an email might land in our inbox and annoy us because the tone comes across as aggressive or insulting. 'Okay,' we might think, 'I'm going to shoot off a response and give tit for tat,' which, of course, will serve only to create conflict—whereas making a phone call or simply walking into the sender's office and saying, 'Hey, do you have time for a coffee? I just wanted to talk about that email you sent ...' could defuse a potentially explosive situation. You would almost certainly find that, when you were face to face with the person, the tone of the communication would be quite different. What could so easily have ended in conflict became an opportunity for improving your relationship with a colleague or direct report.

This illustrates how we often ascribe fears and non-realities to things that don't exist, but we don't know that until we confront them.

As we saw in Chapter 1, if we are conflict avoidant or haven't worked on our ability to manage conflict, we lose sight of the potential benefits of conflict. In terms of Tuckman's stages of group development, which we referred to in Chapter 1, the second stage, storming, where members of the group voice their opinions and conflict arises in the form of disagreements of personality clashes, is a very important part of the group development process. But it can only work if leaders understand that, are able to see what is happening during this stage, and have the courage to direct the conflict rather than either stifling or avoiding it.

This is why it is important to figure out a way to navigate conflict as a team, as an organization, as human beings, so that we are able to be able to recover from it faster. Days at work can feel very long, and there are always highs as well as lows. And when you are experiencing these lows, when you are facing conflict, it can feel like you are taking a punch to the head or to the gut. Metaphorically speaking, part of informed leadership is learning how to take a punch and come back from it stronger and fitter.

Part of informed leadership is learning how to take a punch and come back from it stronger and fitter.

When it comes to decision paralysis, whose causes we investigated in Chapter 1, we need to foster a culture in which people are not publicly shamed for making decisions that turn out to be wrong. Hindsight is a wonderful thing, and it is all too easy to say after the event, 'We should have done this' or 'We shouldn't have done that.' The reality is that nobody can see into the future and we must all make decisions based on the best information we have now. We are not aiming for infallible leadership, but informed leadership.

Accountability as an aid to development

In Chapter 1, I talked about the dangers of performance rating everyone in your team a 4 or 5 out of 5 and of having no clear guidelines across departments and across leaders as to what justifies a 5 or what is required of someone to achieve a 5. Consistency across leadership is essential if performance is to be properly measured and improved.

Part of this process is holding people accountable for poor performance. If we don't, as we have seen, they will assume that all is well and simply jog along at the level they are at, with no urge or incentive to do any better.

Many line managers are reluctant to hold their people accountable for fear of hurting their feelings and making them resentful and, consequently, even worse performing. But, as we have seen, failing to give your direct reports meaningful feedback on their performance leaves them unclear where they stand and what they should and shouldn't be doing. We should therefore not regard holding people to account as 'hurting their feelings', but about course correcting them so that they can better meet the organization's KPIs and thereby benefit themselves as well as the organization as a whole.

We should therefore not regard holding people to account as 'hurting their feelings', but about course correcting them so that they can better meet the organization's KPIs.

To do this, we must have regular talks with our employees, or at least timely conversations when such course correction is required. I often see line managers who are constantly underwhelmed by their direct reports' quality of work and output. But when I ask them the simple question, 'How often do you actually sit down and work with these people and give them feedback?' the common answer I get is, 'Well, every time we have a performance appraisal ...' But performance appraisals usually take place only once or twice a year. If we are going to manage performance effectively, there needs to be a stronger feedback loop in place that enables depth of understanding to take place.

And we need to be able to navigate those conversations in an effective manner so that the receiver, the direct report, is able to see clearly what is expected of them and what the quality of their work needs to look like. In that way, accountability becomes developmental rather than detrimental.

Similarly, when it comes to 'office politics', it is a case of learning how to identify it and deprive it of the oxygen that allows it to breathe, because the more it is allowed to breathe, the more it is going to grow—like a cancer. And just as it is easier to treat a cancer that is at Stage 1 or Stage 2 than one that has been left to progress to Stage 3 or 4, it is much more difficult to neutralize office politics once they have become an accepted modus operandi. The same applies to a silo mentality: Once it has taken root, it is extremely difficult to dislodge it.

When I work with a leader and their team, it is not uncommon for us to notice that there are people on the team that are not pulling their weight, or not performing to the level that is required of that role for the success of the organization. The challenge then becomes deciding whether to address that poor performance and try to bring it up to scratch or simply to replace that individual.

The latter course is, of course, no simple matter. First, you need to have a very good reason for dismissing them. Then you must give them notice and find, recruit, and onboard a replacement, which can take anywhere between three and six months—*if* you are able to find someone who will accept your offer. Even then, since you are at the mercy of the marketplace, you cannot be sure that the person you hire is going to be any better at the job.

I have empathy for leaders in this situation, because there is no easy solution. I often get asked, 'What should I do?'. My answer is almost always, 'You've got to work with what you have.' That means monitoring performance more closely and providing regular feedback.

Distress vs. eustress

We all experience stress at work but, again, there is negative stress and positive stress. Negative stress is bad for us because it causes distress; *positive* stress, known as eustress, is the kind of stress that is good for us. Instead of breaking us, it grows us.

We often talk about post-traumatic stress, less often about its flipside, post-traumatic growth. In 2008, I was involved in a severe car crash and, as a result, almost lost the use of my left hand, which is my dominant hand. For the next six years I was in and out of hospitals, having to have a total of nine operations and countless hours of physio and occupational therapy.

We often talk about post-traumatic stress, less often about its flipside, post-traumatic growth.

At the time, the accident seemed catastrophic. But it had a positive aspect. It forced me to slow down. Prior to the accident I was a workaholic. I was in the business of busyness. During my recovery, I started to see that I needed to change my way of life. I would be lying if I told you I took the lesson like a champ. I realized that I wasn't as resilient or as resourceful as I had thought I was, which is a tough situation to be in. I had my moments of doubt and rejection, but I navigated it. And it was in those moments that I learned the most about myself.

I now believe that if we can enter into the most challenging moments of our life with the awareness that this is an opportunity to really look at ourselves and take a deep dive into who we really are, we will see that there is room for growth. If we are never tested in our lives, we may never know who we are. We can presume who we are, we can say that we believe in certain things, but it is only when we are severely tested that we really find out.

So when I look back at that car crash now, I realize that it opened up the potential for growth in a way that I could not have foreseen. In fact, had I not had that experience, I don't think my career—personal as well as professional—would have taken the same trajectory as it has done.

That was a case of eustress.

If we, as leaders, are able to educate ourselves and understand the difference between distress and eustress, we will be better placed to decide when and how to jump in and support people on our team and when to sit back and let them experience the kind of stress that will enable them to grow and develop. Not knowing the difference is crucial and fundamental, as it can lead us to overcompensate or overreact, which may cause more harm than good.

Seeing beyond the 'leadership bullshit'

There is a lot of advice out there on how to be a better leader—so much, in fact, that it is hard to discern what is good advice and what is not. In his 2015 book *Leadership BS*,[8] Jeffrey Pfeffer challenges many commonly accepted ideas and explodes several myths about leadership. He also calls out certain widely regarded leadership gurus, such as Bill George, author of *True North* and *Authentic Leadership*, having talked to people who worked at Medtronic during George's tenure there as its CEO and heard them describe his leadership style as very different from what he prescribes in those books.

What Pfeffer shows is that a lot of leadership theories are set up in ideal conditions, like laboratory experiments. But real life is not like a laboratory. When you go live in a business situation and try something out for the first time, almost nothing goes according to plan. As Mike Tyson famously said, 'Everybody has a plan until they get punched in the mouth.'

A lot of leadership theories are set up in ideal conditions, like laboratory experiments. But real life is not like a laboratory.

Successful leadership is about being able to make adjustments to your plans as the real-life situation evolves, about being able to adapt, improvise, and overcome, as the old military phrase goes. The world is not black and white, and working within an organization is extremely complex and challenging. Organizations today are plagued with a pace of change that is too fast to track, with strategies that are constantly being challenged, and a volume of ad hoc activities that is increasing day by day, which throws off our ability to be strategic, consistent, and disciplined.

---

8   Jeffrey Pfeffer, *Leadership BS: Fixing Workplaces and Careers One Truth at a Time* (New York, HarperBusiness, 2015).

The only way to navigate this environment is to get ourselves in the right shape and in the right frame of mind with the right skillset to meet that challenge. Simply adopting leadership gurus' prescriptions wholesale, without doing your due diligence, is probably not the best way to go about it. We need a different kind of approach. We need to get back to basics.

A first principles approach

Before we can solve problems at the organizational level, we must go back to the foundations of leadership and understand what it is built upon, its fundamental principles. To introduce these, I must go back to my own beginnings.

Growing up in a poor neighborhood of New York City—the South Bronx in the late 1980s and early 1990s, which was probably one of its most dangerous periods, I observed what might be termed a 'ghetto fab' lifestyle, where outward appearance meant everything, no matter what kind of squalor you might actually be living in. It never made sense to me.

At the same time, it wasn't lost on me that the percentage of people born into poverty who find a way out of it is quite small. But I also realized that one of the main reasons for this is a kind of learned helplessness, whereby people are taught to stay inside their cocoons because they are familiar and safe. As Rita says in Willy Russell's play *Educating Rita*, 'it's really tempting to go out and get another dress, 'cos it's easy ... it doesn't upset anyone around you.'

These experiences taught me very early the importance of believing in ourselves. Like Rita, I was fascinated by the realization that I had a choice. I could choose to stay as I was or to change. In choosing to change and designing my own future path through life, I noticed that the people who had come from where I came from and who had found their way out of poverty, who had managed to transform their lives for the better and create generational wealth, had a few things in common. They all displayed dignity, integrity, respect, and empathy for themselves and for others.

I should say that it took me a while. It wasn't exactly clear to me in the beginning, but one day—it was probably in the early 90s—I found myself in a part of New York City they call midtown, where everyone wore suits and ties and was carrying briefcases. I looked at them and I remember thinking, 'Just because I'm not wearing a suit doesn't mean I'm of no value.' It doesn't matter how much money they make, it doesn't matter what their title is at work, it doesn't matter what kind of honorifics surround their names; they are no better than me.

I knew, however, that the ability to hold myself with dignity was something that I would have to architect for myself. And in doing that for myself, I would also have to hold the people I came into contact with in a dignified manner and treat them like human beings.

It is just the same in organizations. As I have suggested, there is a lot of learned helplessness as a behavior output in organizations, which contributes to an inability to change and transform. So when I say that there is a better way of doing things, I should emphasize that one of the things we have to move past is this learned helplessness. In doing so, we build ourselves up—our leadership profile, our leadership capacity—on a solid foundation.

There is a lot of learned helplessness as a behavior output in organizations, which contributes to an inability to change and transform.

Similar realizations came to me with regard to integrity, respect, and empathy, even though each of them unfolded in different ways. The fact that I was living in a neighborhood infested by gangs and drug use and all kinds of unspeakable tragedies didn't mean that I couldn't live with integrity. It didn't mean that I couldn't hold other people that I came into contact with to my own standards of integrity. Receiving this treatment was their God-given human right.

Coming to this clarity and understanding against one of the most destitute backgrounds a young person can grow up in has helped me to see a way through the complexities of organizational leadership and to shape the principles that I will outline in Part 2 of this book.

Summary

In theory, senior leaders should be looking at long-term financial sustainability; in reality, they are often 'persuaded' to focus on quick wins and short-term successes. In the process, they tend to lose sight of things that are 'part of the fabric' of the organization, that are permitted and thereby promoted. Increasing awareness of these tendencies is paramount. Key to this is an acceptance of conflict and a realization that a commitment to accountability is an essential part of development. Stress at work is inevitable, but this too can have a positive effect—eustress as opposed to distress—enabling us to grow.

We must see through the 'leadership bullshit' notion that we can simply apply a system that will solve all our problems and, instead, adopt a first principles approach that will take us past the learned helplessness inherent in any organization and enable us to build up both ourselves and our direct reports on a solid foundation.

PART TWO

The Foundation Of Informed Leadership

To become an informed leader we must build off a solid foundation. In construction, there is no building without a solid foundation. We may overlook this because the foundation is the most tedious piece of the outwardly looking structure that others can see. But without a foundation, it is like building a house upon sand. And a house upon sand doesn't last. So, while it might not look sexy, getting your foundation right is imperative.

In my work with clients, I always start by asking them, 'What is your foundation? Do you have one? What are the foundational elements that create the baseline you are continuously building upon?'. I tell them I am going to 'shake the trees' and, if something is loose, it is going to fall. If nothing is loose, the trees will remain steady. In other words, if, as soon as something volatile or ambiguous takes place, you fall apart, it shows that your foundation is not solid.

So ask yourself: 'Do I fall apart when the going gets tough? Do I lose sight of my direction when things become foggy or unclear?'. If the answer to those questions is yes, then it is likely you don't have a solid foundation. It doesn't necessarily mean that you don't have elements of a foundation, but there still needs to be work in terms of laying the cement and letting it dry so that it sets, so that it becomes immovable—a base that allows you to be grounded, even in the most trying of times.

In this part of the book I will describe my foundation, which consists of four pillars: respect, integrity, dignity, and empathy. For me, these four pillars are essential to ensuring that the 'structure' of your organization, of your team, is solid. It is these pillars that underpin the primary relationship between line manager and direct report.

To illustrate both the challenges and the ways of overcoming them, I have created a fictitious organization called Company X, whose CEO has just retired, leaving a host of issues for their replacement to deal with …

3
Respect

The first foundation is respect. The OED defines respect as 'due regard for the feelings, wishes, or rights of others.' There is something about that definition that has always spoken to me, and I regularly return to it. I think it is the word 'due' that resonates with me—because everyone is due respect, everyone deserves to be respected, no matter what they look like or what their views are. Respect is simply acknowledging that there is another human being in front of you, imperfect as they may be. It is valuing their hopes and their aspirations. It is acknowledging their right to be themselves, to be unique, to be different from you. Even people we categorize as 'difficult' have the right to be respected for their humanity.

Everyone deserves to be respected, no matter what they look like or what their views are.

Yet we can have trouble respecting other people, because we get so wrapped up in our own lives, our own cares and concerns, that we sometimes don't even see them, let alone take the time to give them due respect. As we saw in Chapter 1, one of the main reasons why people leave their jobs is lack of respect from their line managers, which can be manifested in different ways.

The other side

For this reason the question of respect often comes up in the conversations I have with clients in a coaching or advisory context. In an organizational transformation workshop, for example, once we have built up sufficient trust and psychological safety for participants to open up and vent their frustrations, they will tell me about someone who they feel is the bane of their existence at work. They will go so far as to (quietly) try to enroll me into their way of thinking, and I have to correct myself and remind them that the person they are referring to is also human. When 'they'—the person who is the bane of their existence at work— goes home, someone is happy to see them; it may be a spouse or a child running to the front door, but someone is embracing them, someone values them. They deserve respect.

It is all too easy, if you don't get on with someone, simply to step on them or say that they are wrong. Think instead of what is felt by those people who are excited to see them at the end of the day or sad to say goodbye to them when they go off to work. How is it that they have the complete opposite experience to you when they are with this person? What is going on 'on the other side'?

It is all too easy, if you don't get on with someone, simply to step on them or say that they are wrong.

That is not to say that we shouldn't vent our frustrations. On the contrary, it is healthy to vent, because if you push those frustrations down, they are likely to come back up with even greater force, making it all the more difficult for us to manage them as a result; and if we bottle them up, we tend to ruminate on them, which causes us (and others) pain. We are all human. We need to release our frustrations. What we should avoid doing is blaming other people for those frustrations. One of the first questions I usually ask my clients is, 'How often are you othering people you find difficult to work with?'.

I suggest that we describe them as 'different' rather than 'difficult'. They might not think the way we do, they might not have the same priorities, but they are human beings, just like us, with similar values: They want—and deserve—to be valued and respected. So the next question I ask is, 'Can you suspend your judgment of people who are different from you and spend enough time with them to arrive at a place where you can see their humanity?'. You don't necessarily have to agree with what they are saying, but you should respect that they have a right to their opinion and a right to exist.

A two-way process

Respect goes two ways. However, the balance of power dynamic skews the relationship in the direction of the line manager, which is something we must be aware of. It means that the onus is on leaders to establish the conditions for respect by modeling a respectful attitude toward our direct reports.

If as leaders we are to set up our direct reports for success, we must treat them like adults and not like children. The previous CEO of Company X would often address their C-suite team like a parent talking to a child—and this was no ordinary team, but a 'dream team' that had been carefully assembled, people who were extraordinarily good at what they did. Yet they were treated like children and even, in some cases, as less than human.

If as leaders we are to set up our direct reports for success, we must treat them like adults and not like children.

When we talk about respect, we are talking not only about respect for ourselves and other people and a respectful relationship between line manager and direct reports, but also about respect for the role and the remit of a leader. We must own that we are accountable. We must ask ourselves: Why did we say yes to this role? If our answer is, 'To gain status, a title, an increased salary,' it is clear that we have said yes for the wrong reasons.

There is an old saying that I associate with Peter Parker's uncle Ben in the Spider-Man comics, but which actually originated much earlier:[9] 'With great power comes great responsibility.' You cannot have one without the other and, if you are only exerting your power without accepting your responsibility, you are not respecting your role. And if you are not respecting the role, you may be doing untold damage to your team and to your organization as a whole.

Behavior and culture

If your direct reports see that you, as their leader, are merely exerting the power that comes with your role, the message they will get is: 'This is what leadership looks like.' You will be giving them a definition of leadership that doesn't work.

---

9   Sometimes attributed to Voltaire, the concept can in fact be traced right back to the Bible and the Prophet Muhammad.

When we look again at those statistics on why people leave their jobs (see Chapter 1), we can deduce that one of the reasons is that people are being promoted into leadership positions who are not accepting their responsibility to lead, but only exercising their power as leaders, which is setting the stage for toxic workplaces that lead to increasing levels of stress and disengagement, not to mention burnout and mental health issues.

As I keep repeating (and I make no apology for doing so), what we permit is what we promote. If there is toxicity at the top, it will permeate through the organization. If junior people in an organization see that the way to get promoted is to throw your weight around, that is what they will do (as soon as they have an opportunity to do so). This in turn creates a culture in which it is difficult to be someone who is anything but what is expected, so that even people who are ethically aligned, who have a strong moral compass, will become vulnerable to 'corruption'.

If junior people in an organization see that the way to get promoted is to throw your weight around, that is what they will do.

We cannot be okay with toxicity and, at the same time, claim to respect ourselves and others. The two simply don't align. If we accept toxicity, there is necessarily an absence of respect.

Navigating conflict

The previous CEO of Company X didn't like to give feedback. One of the reasons for this was that they were uncomfortable with being asked questions. Even a fair question such as 'What could I have done differently?' they would take as a personal criticism, as if their judgment was being questioned. They would often simply 'blow up', as if to say, 'I'm not going to be questioned. What I say goes and that's it.'

When I researched the previous CEO's background, I didn't see the necessary 'stepping stones' along the way to becoming a senior leader; there was too much missing leadership experience. They had had several promotions after being in a role for just one or two years, which meant that the skills and the discipline needed to be a chief executive were absent. In terms of readiness and fit for the role, they were an anomaly.

It wasn't simply that they weren't doing their job properly; it was that their lack of conscious strategic leadership development had created too big a gap for them to be successful in the role. Nor did they have the discipline to close that gap. So they were functioning at the 'operational' level of a junior leader.

This is not to say that it is easy to be the chief executive of an organization of any size. It is hard, because the buck stops with you. The real problem, however, is that too many leaders today are not 'fit for purpose'—and most of them know it. According to recent Korn Ferry statistics, over 70% of CEOs in the US suffer from imposter syndrome.[10] The fact that they are leading a big organization doesn't mean that they have the necessary skills, or even the right aspirations, to do so.

In many cases, this is because the organizations they are leading fail to provide them with the appropriate developmental support along their upward path to the top job. In most sports, there is a structure that provides aspiring athletes with a

---

10   Morgan Smith, "71% of CEOs in the U.S. say they have imposter syndrome: 'It's a crisis of confidence'," *CNBC Make It*, June 7 2024, https://www.cnbc.com/2024/06/07/71percent-of-ceos-in-the-us-say-they-have-imposter-syndrome-says-new-report.html (Accessed March 25, 2025).

'ladder', with each rung placing them in the ideal situation to build on their strengths while minimizing their exposure to their weaknesses until the skills gap that created the 'weakness' is no longer a hindrance to their performance. At each stage they take new risks, but these are always calculated, strategic ones. They have a chance of losing, but the likelihood is small. By the time they reach the top rung, they are polished performers— prize fighters, to use the boxing term.

Few organizations have such a system in place (though some are better at providing this than others). Consequently, many of those who rise through the leadership ranks have had little deliberate practice. (We will be returning to the question of deliberate practice in Chapter 7.) This is partly due to the impatience of board members, who get their direction from shareholders. Such reliance encourages short-term results and a 'quick fix' to the organization's problems, placing a lot of pressure on its leaders.

There is often a lack of deliberate practice in connection with ambition when it comes to rising up the ranks in leadership.

Whatever the reasons, if we lack the skills to navigate conflict, we tend to try to avoid it. But the more we try to avoid something, the more we actually draw it to ourselves. In the long run, there is no way to avoid conflict; instead, we must meet it head on and manage it. Otherwise, it will permeate every aspect of our lives, personal as well as professional.

As we have seen, however, managing conflict is a difficult skill to develop. Having a conversation with someone without leaving room for misunderstanding or misinterpretation is not at all easy. At every turn, there is an opportunity for the conversation to go sideways and create tension, leading to greater conflict.

It is up to us to be aware not only of our own lack of skill in this area, but also of other people's. They too may be poor at managing conflict; their mindset may be simply, 'Oh, it's this or that person's fault,' blaming everyone else for the situation they find themselves in, rather than looking at what their own contribution to it was and what they could have done, or might do, differently.

Most of the situations we find ourselves in are 'caused' at least partly by us—whether intentionally or accidentally, consciously or unconsciously. If we are continually finding ourselves in situations where we feel threatened or provoked, it is likely that this is due in some measure to our own weakness. Instead of blaming others, we should therefore assess our own contribution to the situation and seek to overcome that weakness. In other words, we need to respect ourselves and our responsibility, whether as a leader or as a direct report.

Instead of blaming others, we should therefore assess our own contribution to the situation and seek to overcome that weakness.

The inner child

I am in the privileged position of being able to enter an organization with the trust of the senior sponsor—often either the CEO or the chair of the board—and try to help transform or turn a pretty miserable situation into a happy and positive one. People are often at war prior to my arrival, blaming one another and feeling disrespected and undervalued. One of the questions I am often asked is, 'How can someone in such a position behave like a child?'.

My answer is usually along these lines: 'Well, unless they are consciously developing their skills in conflict management or, as we say in the world of personal development, unless they are doing their work—which never ends—they are likely to perpetually behave like the child they were when they learned the defense mechanism of either avoiding or protecting themselves from conflict.'

We learn those behaviors between the ages of around five and eight; any time we feel scared or threatened as adults, we resort to that mechanism for protection. It is as if we were trying to function in a Windows 10 environment using a Windows 95 operating system. And unless we are consciously aware that this is happening, we unconsciously allow it to continue metastasizing in our behavior. You might have gone to an Ivy League school or an Oxbridge university; you might have a Master's or a PhD; it makes no difference. The moment you are triggered, you are likely to go back to your childhood.

If we haven't done our work, we are not even aware of this, let alone able to do anything about it. Knowing this is the first step toward accepting it and appreciating the importance of respect. It is part of our responsibility as leaders.

Fighting right

We have seen why avoiding conflict is a common strategy. We have also seen that, in doing so, Company X's previous CEO succeeded only in exacerbating that conflict. There is another option—one that aligns with our responsibility to respect our direct reports, ourselves, and our role as leaders. It is to 'fight right'.

The term comes from marriage counseling, but it applies to any human relationship, because the dynamics within a marriage also show up within teams in the relationships between a line manager and their direct reports. Whether they are intimate or professional, relationships are governed by human emotions and/or emotional maturity, which is the same in all contexts.

> *Whether they are intimate or professional, relationships are governed by human nature and/or emotional maturity, which is the same in all contexts.*

When couples are in a state of paralysis, it is important to set up a process for working their way out of it and a roadmap showing what each phase in that process looks like, so that the couple is able to see a solution to their problems and a way forward from a situation that seems impossible to resolve. That way, they can start to have confidence in the process and feel able to participate in the resolution.

Fighting right is about getting clear on what is acceptable and what is not acceptable. And that requires courage. In fact, it requires everything that we have discussed so far. It requires dignity, integrity, and above all respect. Respect for our 'opponent'.

I am reminded of the Ron Howard movie *Rush*, which tells the story of the rivalry between F1 drivers James Hunt and Niki Lauda in the 1980s. It beautifully shows that neither could have reached the heights they did if it had not been for the other, pushing them to the limit—an important thing to remember when we are prone to denigrating and blaming our professional 'opponents'.

If we look at conflict through this lens, we see that there is a healthiness to the tension inherent in it. If we can leverage it the right way, we have an opportunity to push ourselves— and our opponents—past our limits. If we can harness that potential within our organization, we can create a competitive advantage in the marketplace.

Doing so demands respect. It requires us to recognize that the fact that someone disagrees with you doesn't necessarily mean they are wrong. Nor does it mean that they are necessarily disrespecting or criticizing you. There are situations where both parties, who may be at opposite ends of an agreement, are right. It just depends on the way you look at things. We generally look at things from our own perspective. What we also need to do is look at them from other people's points of view.

When I am working with leaders or with teams that are in conflict and we are discussing how to fight right and create a protocol for resolving the conflict, I often start with John Stuart Mill's words: 'He who knows only his own side of the case, knows little of that. His reasons may be good, and no one may have been able to refute them. But if he is equally unable to refute the reasons on the opposite side; if he does not so much as know what they are, he has no ground for preferring either opinion.'[11]

I would even go further and say that, in arguing the merits of the other side, you will strengthen your understanding of your own side. You may also arrive at a synthesis of the two sides, which is stronger than either.

Going back to the field of marriage counseling, leading expert in the field of relationship dynamics Esther Perel describes the flow of relationships as a three-step process: There is calm, there is chaos, and then there is repair. This is the natural ebb and flow of a relationship dynamic; you cannot always have calm, because harmony without disruption is just not possible.

There are natural processes in all things. The seasons progress from summer to fall to winter to spring and back to

---

11   J. S. Mill, "On Liberty" (Bobbs-Merrill, 1859).

summer, and there is tension when one season gives way to the next, when one takes over from the last. It is unavoidable, just as we cannot avoid conflict. What we can do is understand what the dance looks like and that there is an ebb and a flow in relationships that we can navigate.

We must understand that there is an ebb and a flow in relationships that we can navigate.

Looking in the mirror

My way of checking in on myself, my litmus test for how I am doing—a technique I learned when I lived in South Korea—is simply to look at myself in the mirror. If I can hold my gaze it is a good sign, because it means that I like what I see reflected back to me. But if I cannot hold my gaze for more than a few seconds, I know that something is not right.

It takes a certain amount of courage and honesty to look at yourself and see what is there. If we aren't honest with ourselves, we cannot expect others to respect us. As leaders we must make ourselves aware of the gaps in our understanding, in our abilities, and what we need to do to fill them. This is part of the social contract we make when we take on the role of a leader. As I have said, with great power comes great responsibility; and if we aren't able to accept that, we are in the wrong job.

It takes a certain amount of courage and honesty to look at yourself and see what is there.

No one is perfect, no one is always right, no one is always wrong, and no one can be expected to know everything, but as leaders we are expected to revisit our capabilities and ask ourselves regularly, 'Am I doing the best I can? Or could I do better?'. If we aren't asking ourselves those questions, we are not respecting ourselves, we are not respecting others, and we are not respecting our role.

Summary

Respect means 'due regard for the feelings, wishes, or rights of others.' Everyone deserves to be respected, and we should avoid blaming others for our frustrations. If we have trouble working with someone, we should regard them as 'different' rather than 'difficult'.

Referring to the state of leadership as a form of othering is not a solution-oriented strategy either. Yes, there is a place for critics to voice their concerns and provide data to serve as a checks-and-balances system, but the point remains the same: The othering of leaders only furthers the distance between what is and what could be.

We must also have respect for the role of a leader. 'With great power comes great responsibility.' It is not a case of merely exerting the power that comes with the role, which is merely to revert to childhood defense mechanisms. We must be clear on what is acceptable and what is not acceptable and see that there is a healthiness to conflict, which can push people, including ourselves, beyond our limits and create competitive advantage for our organization.

As leaders, we must assess our own contribution to a situation and make ourselves aware of the gaps in our understanding and what we need to do to fill them—to ask ourselves regularly, 'Am I doing the best I can? Or could I do better?'.

4

Integrity

According to the Oxford English Dictionary,[12] there are two definitions of integrity: 'The quality of being honest and having strong moral principles' and 'The state of being whole and undivided.' The first of these means having a strong ethical GPS system, so to speak, that tells us what is right and what is wrong. In this sense, I like to think of integrity as doing the right thing when no one is looking.

I like to think of integrity as doing the right thing when no one is looking.

The second definition is normally applied to inanimate objects, but for me it is equally, if not more, important in relation to the

12 Oxford English Dictionary, "Integrity", www.oed.com/dictionary/integrity_n?tl=true, accessed March 27, 2025.

qualities required of a leader. If we are 'whole and undivided', we are consistent and we know who we are and who we are not. We are comfortable in our own skin. We may be under an enormous amount of pressure and experiencing intense stress, but we have sufficient sense of self to be able to navigate it. It doesn't necessarily mean that we are going to win, but we are in a position to give it our best shot.

When I started digging into the legacy of the last CEO at Company X, I soon discovered part of the problem they had left behind was due to a lack of integrity.

It turned out that, when the organization had sought to appoint a new COO—the position having been vacant for some time, during which the CEO had been fulfilling both roles—they had sanctioned the appointment of a person with whom they were having an ongoing personal relationship. Rather than being upfront and declaring the relationship, and thereby recusing themselves from the hiring process, the former CEO had kept it secret and even voted in favor of the person being taken on.

Worse, the CEO then okayed an increase in the salary offer for the role—over and above the agreed budget—when that person requested it. All this despite the fact that the person in question was unfit for the role of COO.

Over the first couple of months after the appointment, it began to come to light that the new COO and the CEO had an ongoing relationship—whenever there was a meeting of the senior management team, for example, a certain 'dynamic' was apparent, and the CEO would criticize others but never the COO—but it wasn't until four months after the COO had been hired that the truth came out.

This situation had several adverse effects. It created distrust among the senior management team. It became difficult for them to collaborate on an even basis, because the COO felt that they were above everyone else and would talk down to them or try to dominate peer-level projects. If they didn't get their way, they would go to the CEO and say, 'Hey, this person's giving me trouble,' and the CEO would come down hard on that other person.

It also created a misalignment in terms of relationships. If the COO had been asked about their relationship with the CEO, they would almost certainly have given glowing feedback. But if the remaining C-suite members had been asked what their relationship was like with the CEO, they would probably have given an entirely different set of feedback. Both could be 'true' from the point of view of the people concerned, but these truths would be fundamentally inconsistent.

What we are seeing here is that the absence of integrity eroded the foundation for that team to work effectively together.

The trust equation

We have seen the importance of consistency. In this situation, there was obvious inconsistency in the way that the CEO was dealing with members of their team, which led to an absence of trust.

In *The Trusted Advisor*,[13] the authors set out what they call a 'trust equation':

$$Trust = \frac{credibility + reliability + intimacy}{self\text{-}interest}$$

---

13   Charles H. Green, Robert M. Galford, and David H. Maister (Simon and Schuster, 2001).

Let us look at each of the four elements in the equation in turn.

Credibility means, essentially, having the background to do the thing that you have been tasked to do. If, for example, someone is heading up an aviation business yet has no background in aviation or related areas, like engineering, logistics, or transportation, it will be very difficult for experts in that area to fall into line under that person. He or she will lack credibility. In our fictitious situation in Company X, the COO lacked credibility because they were not qualified or able to fulfill the functions of that role.

Reliability is simply doing what you are tasked to do or doing what you say you are going to do, when you are required or when you say you are going to do it. In this respect, it is closely related to consistency. If you have a deadline at the end of the week or the close of business and you push it at the last minute, or if you are constantly behind schedule or failing to do what you say you are going to do, it will be very difficult for others to engage with you as a partner, because you lack reliability. In Company X, it became very difficult to be line-managed by the previous CEO because they were inconsistent and unreliable.

Intimacy is a rather more problematic item in the equation. We tend to think of intimacy in a physical sense, but in this context it points to the depth or the substance of a business relationship. There are no two ways about it: Business is personal. We spend more time in our lives with our colleagues than we do with our own families. This doesn't mean that we need to love the people we work with, but we mustn't minimize the importance of business relationships and kid ourselves that we can compartmentalize relationships at work. Relationships—all relationships—matter.

There are no two ways about it: Business is personal.

A recent study into employee retention,[14] which is a major contributing factor to risk mitigation and continuity within an organization, showed that a key determinant of whether someone in a tough work environment is likely to persist and be retained is whether or not they have a 'best friend' at work— someone you can lean into, someone who has got your back. A measure of this, for example, is whether, if you are not at work one day, anyone calls you to check that you are okay.

Emotional support from a 'best friend' at work creates a sense of intimacy. Therefore, anything less intensive than this will not reflect the depth of relationship needed to create emotional intimacy, because it unbalances the trust equation by putting self-interest above the other elements.

In simple terms, self-interest is having skin in the game for something that we want. This is where the equation gets tricky, because everyone wants something. Everyone has some kind of self-interest. However, if trust is important to you as a business leader, it is up to you to ensure that your self-interest is not greater than your credibility, reliability, and intimacy. If the self-interest equation works out at >1, you won't achieve trust. You won't come across as having integrity.

If trust is important to you as a business leader, it is up to you to ensure that your self-interest is not greater than your credibility, reliability, and intimacy.

---

14 Alok Patel and Stephanie Plowman, "The Increasing Importance of a Best Friend at Work," *Gallup Workplace*, August 17, 2022, https://www.gallup.com/workplace/397058/increasing-importance-best-friend-work.aspx#:~:text=Gallup%20data%20indicate%20that%20having,safety%2C%20inventory%20control%20and%20retention (accessed March 27, 2025).

For the previous CEO at Company X, trust was a nice-to-have, but it wasn't essential. Their own self-interest was too important for that ... They didn't have integrity in the way we have defined it, which meant that the problems the succeeding CEO inherited should not have come as a surprise. The former CEO was seen to have put self-interest above credibility, reliability, and intimacy; so, inevitably, everyone reporting to them did the same. What we permit is what we promote.

If we have too much self-interest, what is going to happen is that the other person will feel used, manipulated, exploited. Let me give you an example.

Senior leaders in an organization can be great mentors for high-performing and ambitious junior people who are looking to climb the corporate ladder. For them, choosing the right mentor can accelerate their career dramatically, because a good mentor not only helps them to see the way forward, but they have also been there and done it themselves. A good mentor–mentee relationship, where the mentor is really invested in the mentee's development, can also provide valuable introductions and networking opportunities, and even an insight into high-level negotiations such as a merger or MOU.

What often happens, however, is that a mentee will seek out a mentor for the sole purpose of promotion—a 'soft touch' such as a senior manager who is nearing retirement and winding down their own career. If this happens, the mentor can feel that the relationship is not natural or authentic, that they are merely being used. In such a situation, self-interest outweighs credibility, reliability, and intimacy; the trust equation 'doesn't add up', and there is a lack of integrity.

This is because trust must work both ways: It is not only our direct reports who must trust us; we must also trust them.

Short-term vs long-term discomfort

The previous CEO of Company X was well aware of the lack of trust on their team—caused largely by their undisclosed relationship with the new COO. They realized that this lack of trust was creating tension among people on the team and making it much more difficult to work together. However, the CEO also knew that rectifying the situation would require a huge, long-term commitment. But the CEO had only a year left before retirement. So instead of making the effort, they simply left things the way they were, accepted the existing situation and kept pushing through with whatever initiatives they saw as important for the business. The cost of trying to tackle the issue of transforming the senior management to function as a high-performing team was just not something they were willing to get behind. Okay, there would be short-term discomfort along the way and that would eventually pile up into long-term discomfort, but that would be for the next CEO to handle. Not their problem.

This attitude clearly showed that the former CEO lacked integrity. But when I started delving into the history of Company X, I learned that they hadn't always been like that.

Humanizing the other

I learned that the former CEO had once had integrity, but the challenges they had faced had eventually broken their back. As CEO, their remit had covered not just one organization but a whole group of organizations, each with its own culture and status quo, and the CEO's ethical system hadn't been sufficiently solid to withstand the pressures that entailed, so that they had eventually been beaten down. And once your back is broken, you no longer want to stick your head up and voice dissenting opinions because you know you are likely to be cut down again.

What came out of this was the importance of humanizing the person you are demonizing—in this case the previous CEO—and finding the reasons why they are the way they are: why they are 'difficult', 'challenging', 'obstructive', 'disengaged', or whatever. People don't behave that way for the hell of it; there is always a reason. Somewhere. It might be buried deep; they might conceal it really well; but it will be there somewhere. And it is up to you, as their leader, to find it, rather than simply to dismiss them as 'a problem' and focus your mind elsewhere.

In his book *How Will You Measure Your Life?*,[15] the late Clayton Christensen references Jeffrey Skilling, the former CEO of Enron, who was convicted of one of the biggest frauds in US business history. It turns out that Skilling was once a friend of Christensen—they were at Harvard together, studying for their MBAs—and the Jeffrey Skilling he knew wasn't the kind of man who would falsify financial documents, let alone knowingly cause a monumental international scandal. So what happened to him along the way? What led someone who was faithful to his wife and a good father to his children down a path that ultimately led to his being incarcerated for 13 years?

Clearly, he didn't always lack integrity. What he obviously *did* lack, though, was a solid ethical operating system founded on dignity, respect, and empathy, as well as integrity, without which we are vulnerable to the intense pressure of occupying a leadership role with a huge remit and major responsibility. And no one is impervious to those vulnerabilities. We must all build up our defenses so as to be able to withstand the onslaught that is the challenge of senior leadership.

---

15   Thorsons (2019).

We must all build up our defenses so as to be able to withstand the onslaught that is the challenge of senior leadership.

Fiduciary duty

When I was still living in New York, I asked a friend who worked in financial services, 'Where do you put your money?'. And they said, 'With The Vanguard Group.' When I asked why, the answer was that they are a fiduciary; they aren't selling anything, they aren't taking a commission, they are just giving people advice based on their needs. It was my introduction to fiduciary duty— and it made perfect sense to me.

Let me be clear: I am not saying that a financial advisor who takes a commission is necessarily a bad person, but naturally an element of self-interest comes into play; and whenever self-interest is in play, the terrain becomes trickier to navigate.

I may be in the minority, but I believe that leaders, regardless of seniority in the organization, are fiduciaries. (Whether or not they see themselves as fiduciaries is a different question, which may be a topic for another book ....) Senior leaders have fiduciary duty over a number of verticals within an organization, and their success lies in their ability to align those verticals so that they work as a collective on behalf of the organization as a whole. What we often find, however, is that a win for one vertical comes at the cost of losses for three other verticals that are supposed to be working cross-functionally together.

Senior leaders have fiduciary duty over a number of verticals within an organization, and their success lies in their ability to align those verticals so that they work as a collective on behalf of the organization as a whole.

More importantly, however, leaders are fiduciaries because they impact a lot of other people—and not just at work. Their influence is far more pervasive than that. Let me give you an example from my own experience, which might at first seem off topic. (Bear with me.)

In the late 90s, when I was an educator, there was a great debate over the influence on children of the time they spent with their parents. Somewhere in the mid-90s, it was finally recognized that it is not so much the quantity of time as the quality of that time that matters.

Imagine, for example, that a parent has come home from work tired, after a tough day (or a tough couple of days or a tough week or a tough month), and they are having dinner with their child. Although the child can see that the parent is tired, the parent is saying and demonstrating through their behavior that they still love what they do, even though things are tough. The parent is not only showing the child what resilience looks like, what it looks like to be committed to something; they are also modeling emotional maturity, the ability to hold two seemingly contradictory things as true: that they can love something that is tough. The child will learn that life, far from being black and white, contains a lot of gray. This realization will lead to better life outcomes, academically, professionally, and socially.

Now imagine another parent coming home tired and defeated. They complain about their work, about their boss, about themselves, about life. What does that teach the child? That everything is doom and gloom—and there is nothing they can do about it. Learned helplessness. And what kind of outcomes are they likely to have in *their* lives?

It has been shown that children in the latter case are more likely to experiment with drugs, to indulge in deviant behavior, to engage in pubescent sex, and, perhaps surprisingly, to bully other children at school.

All of which goes to show the extent of our fiduciary duty as leaders. If we model negativity and helplessness to our direct reports, they will ultimately model the same negativity and helplessness to their children, thus widening the impact of ineffective leadership.

> *If we model negativity and helplessness to our direct reports, they will ultimately model the same negativity and helplessness to their children, thus widening the impact of ineffective leadership.*

As leaders, we do not only have a fiduciary duty to our shareholders and to the planet; we also have a fiduciary duty to our community, to the entire ecosystem of the people we come into contact with and the people they come into contact with. The quality of our relationships with those people will have a significant impact.

In this regard, we should look to leadership specialists such as the Johnson & Johnson Institute in Florida, which, when providing 360-degree feedback to its senior leadership, includes not only their line managers, peers, and direct reports but also their family to gain insight into how they perform at home as well as at work. This reinforces their belief that sustained performance across the board is mission-critical and that no single domain is more important than any other.

We must therefore ask ourselves: 'Am I fully committed to undertaking the due diligence required of my fiduciary duty, or am I just looking to increase my organization's stock prices next month?'.

If that question foxes us, we need to look hard in the mirror and assess our integrity, because, whether we like it or not, whether intentionally or accidentally, we are impacting other people's lives.

Summary

Having integrity means being honest and following strong moral principles, but it also means being whole and undivided. An absence of integrity erodes the foundation for teams to work effectively together. To do so, team members must trust each other. The 'trust equation' is:

$$Trust = \frac{credibility + reliability + intimacy}{self\text{-}interest}$$

It is up to leaders to ensure that their self-interest is not greater than their credibility, reliability, and intimacy. It is not only direct reports who must trust their leaders; their leaders must also trust them. Rather than simply dismissing a 'challenging' employee as 'a problem', we must humanize them and try to understand the causes of their behavior.

As senior leaders we have a fiduciary duty not only over the various verticals within our organization, but also over its people and the people they come into contact with—outside as well as inside the organization. We must look at ourselves in the mirror and ask whether we are fully committed to undertaking the due diligence required of that fiduciary duty.

5

Dignity

The third foundation is dignity, which can be defined simply as the state or quality of being held in honor or respect. To have dignity, you must be able to see yourself as being worthy of honor or respect. It sounds simple and it obviously makes sense, but in today's fast-paced world of work, dignity is no longer a given.

In today's fast-paced world of work, dignity is no longer a given.

If we are unable to manage stress and are unclear of the difference between distress and 'eustress' (a moderate level of stress, beneficial for the individual), our ability to hold ourselves with dignity is already compromised. If there is an absence of accountability and our direct reports are unsure what the expectations are of them from their line managers and leaders (us), how can we expect them to honor or respect us?

So how do we compose ourselves in a manner that reflects dignity?

Walking your talk

First and foremost, we need to be consistent. We must walk our talk. It is no good saying one thing and doing another, because this will only cause confusion and create tension. If we make a verbal commitment to A and B by saying they are important, but then decide to do C and D instead, we create a misalignment, and no one knows what is going on. What we say is devalued, which creates an absence of dignity. If people no longer value what we say, we lose their respect.

If people no longer value what we say, we lose their respect.

The former CEO of Company X would hold update meetings to solicit from their colleagues where a particular project stood in terms of its delivery as well as from a budget perspective. At one such meeting, the CEO agreed with both the COO and the CFO as to the direction that should be taken on an initiative along with the allocation of resources, i.e. budget, but immediately following the meeting, the COO engaged the CEO privately to say that they may need an increased budget. As a result of that conversation, the CEO informed the CFO to raise the budget for the COO on that project. When the CFO asked for justification for the budget amendment, the CEO got upset and told the CFO to 'get on with it' and 'get the details from the COO'.

Instead of trying to be consistent, the CEO was merely being directive. They were too often focused on the end result and didn't want to be bothered with 'unnecessary details'.

They regarded questions and discussions as unnecessary, even disrespectful, and didn't like to be in a meeting for more than 10 minutes—which didn't allow ideas to simmer and settle before being actioned. It was up to them to make decisions and for others to follow instructions. Dignity wasn't even a consideration. It was that lack of attention that created a negative feedback loop.

Of course, everyone has the right to change their mind and ask for a change of direction, especially if some new information comes in that could impact the way things work out, but the reason for the change must be clearly communicated and its potential impacts explained and understood.

On other occasions, after something had been 'agreed' at a meeting, the COO (or another C-suite leader with whom the CEO had a close relationship) would take the CEO aside and influence them to change direction, like in the previous example. Say the COO wanted more budget for a program but didn't want to say so in front of the CFO. Lacking dignity, the CEO might capitulate (to save time) and then tell the CFO to change the budget, even though it had already been 'publicly' approved and allocated.

Ego

Reflecting on the CEO's behavior, it was clear to me that the impulsiveness behind their decision-making was partly connected to ego—a desire to assert themselves and 'justify' their position—and partly to a general sense of unease and lack of confidence. It was out of their comfort zone to allow back and forth with their colleagues, so they would resort to being directive and authoritative—and even avoid being accessible when requested by their C-suite team.

But ego can work the other way, too. If we look at the COO's behavior in the above scenario, for example, we can see that from their perspective their ego wasn't being fed, or even accounted for, by the CEO's leadership method. So they had to resort to 'undignified' tactics, i.e. taking the CEO aside and trying to persuade them to change tack. This would not only get them a bigger budget for their program, but also boost their ego. If the CEO hadn't agreed to increase their budget, it would have hurt the COO's feelings, resulting in them going silent and 'flying under the radar' for days afterward or, worse, becoming petulant and deliberately uncooperative. The CEO knew that, and the COO knew the CEO knew and would be uncomfortable about it—hence the CEO's capitulation and the perpetuation of the accepted modus operandi. As we have seen already, what you permit is what you promote.

This absence of dignity thus allows us to be (mis)led by our egos. But it is not always intentional or malicious; it can also result from a lack of self-awareness. In the heat of the moment, in a meeting of senior people with big responsibilities taking major decisions on behalf of the organization, it can be very difficult to work out whether we are talking and acting within our role as a leader or whether we are being led by our ego. So the challenge is to take the time to reflect on how we are performing, on why we are saying what we are saying and doing what we are doing, so that we are more likely to react to situations intentionally—with intent—rather than unwittingly. When we talk about laying the foundation of dignity, we are really looking at being intentional and aware so that our leadership is more informed as a result.

In the heat of the moment it can be very difficult to work out whether we are talking and acting within our role as a leader or whether we are being led by our ego.

In my talks with the new CEO, we quickly identified the residue of the previous workplace culture and saw why it was creating a malaise at all levels of the organization. So in our initial conversations the question was, 'How do we overcome this and restore some normalcy?'. For me, the only way to do that was for the new CEO to be clear and consistent in their communication. Anything that deviated from a path of clarity and consistency would be a sign of misalignment of purpose; and, as we have seen, misalignment of purpose leads to poor performance and lack of prosperity.

It was, however, not enough for the CEO to be clear and consistent; they must also speak to that new strategy. They must say something like, 'In the past there was a lot of inconsistency and the absence of clarity. Moving forward, what we say needs to mean something because our words have meaning and our words lead to action, and actions have impact on the organization. If we're going to be better at what we do, we need to get that right.'

Interference

In Tim Gallwey's *The Inner Game* series,[16] which many executive coaches consider to be a foundational book for their coaching practices, he constructs a formula for success:

Performance = Potential – Interference.

---

16 See *The Inner Game®*, https://theinnergame.com/ (accessed March 27, 2025).

I discussed this in my conversations with the new CEO and asked: 'What is the interference that is getting in the way of the organization's performance?'. Not: 'Who is to blame for the interference?' but simply, 'What is the interference?'. Because by removing blame, you create objectivity. And if we can create objectivity in the way we see what is going on—what is going right and what is getting in the way—it is less threatening, which leads to a better outcome. Any interference can be addressed constructively, without simply laying it at the feet of the previous CEO.

We could acknowledge that the previous CEO had allowed certain things to metastasize, but it wouldn't serve the current CEO's purpose to throw the previous CEO under the bus, because that in itself is undignified. And if we are trying to move toward behaving with dignity, both holding it for ourselves and holding it for others, we need to be able to model that. Addressing interference in an objective way, as an obstacle to be removed to unlock dignity, is the way forward.

Addressing interference in an objective way, as an obstacle to be removed to unlock dignity, is the way forward.

Discipline

When times get tough, we are often not the best versions of ourselves. We need great discipline to develop and maintain the right habits, to establish and preserve our dignity.

To help guide our understanding of how to do this, we only have to look to the Stoics. It never ceases to amaze me that you can read Epictetus or Marcus Aurelius or Seneca and find that their words apply to today's workplace context, although they were written thousands of years ago. Why do they resonate so? Because their approach is exactly like ours: a return to first principles. They removed all the fat, cut life to the bone, and exposed the root cause of things. And when we look at what propelled the Stoics to become who they were, we see that discipline was central to the way that they operated. Discipline opens the door to consistency. And consistency opens the door to being deliberate and intentional.

Discipline opens the door to consistency. And consistency opens the door to being deliberate and intentional.

Stoicism

If the word 'Stoicism' rubs you the wrong way, let me put you at ease. One of the more common misconceptions of the Stoics is that they were devoid of emotion. In fact, they weren't devoid of emotion; they were human just like us. They were vulnerable to the same sorts of triggers that make us all passionate or angry or envious or indulgent. But they were also aware of what happens when we lose a sense of self and allow our emotions to get the better of us. They understood that, if they could increase their ability to recover from triggered emotions, they would be in a better place to be both functional and contented. To do this they needed to be highly disciplined. The Stoics may not have been perfect, but they provided us with a blueprint that we can still follow today.

To be able to manage our emotions, to find a way to make peace with the flaws in us as human beings, while still aspiring to greatness and excellence, we have to be disciplined. This means focusing on the things that get in our way without judgment or blame, and without feeling guilty about removing them.

Locus of control

The emotional triggers we are subject to include things that we can control and things that we cannot control. Imagine for a minute that you are stuck in traffic. (You probably don't have to use your imagination much.) You have just left work. It is rush hour. You really want to get home—to your partner, your kids, your dog, whatever. But you aren't moving. It frustrates you. It might even make you angry. You might cut lanes or take a detour in an attempt to get home sooner, to assert some influence and control over the situation. But it is unlikely to make any significant difference. The situation is outside your control. It is what it is.

What is within your control is how you react to it. Imagine that, instead of giving in to your frustration, you pull into a gas station or get off at the next exit and have a coffee or read a book or listen to some music or an interesting podcast. You say to yourself, 'You know what? I'm going to enjoy the next half hour. I'm going to make the best use of that time.' That way, you reclaim some of your power over the situation. You retain your dignity.

This is what is meant by recognizing our locus of control; and it is another lesson taught to us thousands of years ago by the Stoics, who focused on what was within their control because that was what they could impact. What is outside our control, we must learn to let go of, as they did.

Two things that can interfere with the performance of your organization are office politics and a silo mentality, as we discussed in Chapter 1. We can see now, however, that these are largely outside our control. In any organization, there are many different types of personalities at work. Some people can be difficult and, dare I say, some are not always 'ethically aligned'. Such types will almost certainly exist within the ecosystem that you operate in. But to get mad about it and rail at the 'politics' or the silo mentality will serve no purpose. Unless you are the senior sponsor of a transformation project that aims to change the way that people work, these things are beyond your control.

What is within your control if you are a leader is the way *you* engage with your team, the quality of *your* conversations with your direct reports, the sense of commitment and collaboration that you foster within your team. Your domain of control is yourself: the way in which you carry yourself, the way in which you treat others. If cross-functionally at your organization, people don't want to play nice, there is nothing you can do; it is beyond your control. So forget about it.

Your domain of control is yourself: the way in which you carry yourself, the way in which you treat others.

On the other hand, if you find that someone within your department, within your team, is being disrespectful or rude, you don't have to stand for that. That *is* within your locus of control, so you must take action: Assert or communicate a boundary with that person so that it doesn't happen again. If it does happen again, even though you have had that conversation with them, you must impose some kind of sanction on them. You might simply limit your contact with them—whether professionally or socially—or you might actively penalize them in some way, not vindictively, but simply to show them that their behavior is unacceptable and will not be 'permitted'.

Beyond that, we cannot control other people; we can only control ourselves. We can impact and influence, but we have to start with ourselves. If we are faced with a situation that is not up to our standard and we look for a solution outside of ourselves instead of within ourselves, we will only be contributing to that problem rather than resolving it.

Hero's journey

No matter where you sit in the organization—whether you lead a team of two or a team of 500—you are on a leadership journey. In *The Hero's Journey*,[17] Joseph Campbell describes his quest for meaning through mythic traditions and rituals, which led him to the realization that regardless of religion and race, regardless of the period of time, regardless of geography, there are these common elements to all humanity's stories: there is a hero, who is confronted by a dragon—real or metaphorical—which represents some kind of obstacle that is in the hero's way, obstructing their path toward growth or self-actualization; and when the hero confronts the dragon, they are scared and tempted to retreat or hide; but, being a hero, they overcome their fear and 'slay the dragon' in their path.

> *The archetypal hero's journey applies to us as leaders of organizations. We will face not one but many 'dragons'.*

This archetypal hero's journey applies to us as leaders of organizations. We will face not one but many 'dragons'. We will be scared and tempted to avoid confrontation or 'put our heads in the sand'. We will see others retreating into a silo mentality or outright disengagement rather than facing the dragon. It is up to us to face up to it, to level up and challenge it head on. When we do so, we become stronger. It reinforces our ability to confront other dragons, whether at work or in life more generally. We have a better sense of self, a greater sense of dignity.

---

17   3rd ed. (New World Library, 2014).

Summary

To hold ourselves with dignity, we must above all be consistent. We must not say one thing and do another, which causes confusion and creates tension. We may change our mind, but we must clearly explain the reasons for doing so. We must also clearly distinguish between acting in our own interests and acting in the interests of the organization we are leading.

Performance = Potential - Interference. We must therefore seek to ascertain what is getting in the way of the organization's performance, rather than blaming anyone for that interference. Addressing interference in an objective way is dignified. When the going gets tough, it requires great discipline to manage our emotions and focus on the things that get in our way without judgment or blame.

We must also distinguish between things that we can control and things that we cannot control. In the latter case, what is within our control is how we react to them. We may not be able to control our direct reports' behavior, but we can control the way we engage with them, the way we carry ourselves, and the way we treat them.

6
Empathy

My preferred definition of empathy comes from the Cambridge Dictionary:[18] 'The ability to share someone else's feelings or experiences by imagining what it would be like to be in that person's situation.' I like it because it makes a crucial distinction between empathy and sympathy.

Showing sympathy—by saying, for example, 'I know how you feel. I'm sorry.'—is a little patronizing and disrespectful. It is rather like saying, 'Yeah, you're in a bad place, but it doesn't feel that dire to me.' You are in a sense hijacking the other person's story, reinterpreting it in your own terms and spewing it back out. They may not even be feeling distressed, but your sympathy makes them feel that way. Worse than that, it is disempowering because you are treating them like a victim.

---

18 Cambridge Dictionary, "Empathy", https://dictionary.cambridge.org/dictionary/english/empathy, accessed March 27, 2025.

With empathy, on the other hand, comes compassion. For example, offering a listening ear to someone who express their struggles with a personal issue at home that has interfered with their performance at work is empathic. To offer or express support only reinforces empathy. You don't have to feel sorry for the other person, and you can still believe in their capacity to navigate through their difficult situation. They may be aggrieved, but they are not helpless. You are showing respect for them, for their dignity and integrity.

We have more in common than we have differences, so that where there are divides, there are always ways to build bridges; but we don't see that unless we are committed to empathy.

The final pillar

This means that, in order to arrive at empathy, you must already have the other three pillars in place. In fact, the more I think about empathy, the more I am convinced that, to get there, you have to go through respect, integrity, and dignity first.

The more I think about empathy, the more I am convinced that, to get there, you have to go through respect, integrity, and dignity first.

For a long time after I first developed the idea of the pillars, there were just three: dignity, integrity, and respect. Then, over the years, my thinking evolved to include empathy. I would be interacting with someone and believing that I was respecting their dignity and integrity but suddenly realizing that I was also silently, or unconsciously, making some kind of judgment against them.

The key element in the equation that was missing was compassion. You can have respect for someone, but if you don't also come to them with compassion, you can only feel sorry for them, which is not enough.

As I have said, when I was growing up, it always puzzled me that people who had no money in their pocket, who couldn't make the rent or put food on the table, who had young children to support, would buy the latest clothes—the most expensive sneakers or an outfit that cost $500. For a long time, I couldn't understand that. I would put those people in a metaphorical box and imagine I was asking them, 'What's wrong with you?'. It wasn't until later that I started to get it. When you don't have access to a university education, which means that you are unlikely to become upwardly mobile but will just move from job to job, you are at risk; you feel like you have no control of your life. You need something to make you feel good about yourself, even if only temporarily, and buying the latest clothes achieves that.

Empathy makes working with people more fruitful, because you are coming to them without judgment—which they will inevitably sense, even if you are unaware of it.

Empathy makes working with people more fruitful, because you are coming to them without judgment—which they will inevitably sense, even if you are unaware of it.

Shared accountability

In Company X, under the former CEO, there were multiple conflicts among members of the C-suite. In one particular conflict, the aggrieved party reached out to the former CEO, asking them to step in and adjudicate the situation because it required a decision from the top. Part of the reason their working relationship had gone sour was that they were trying, unsuccessfully, to make sense of something that hadn't been clarified at the senior level, so that it was hard to tell where role and remit definitions started and ended; the aggrieved was accountable for the output, but the other person was responsible for the project design. So the aggrieved asked the CEO if they could redesign the project so that everyone had a clearer understanding of what shared accountability looked like.

When the aggrieved put this question to the former CEO, however, the latter immediately felt criticized; they took it as a slight and a hit to their ego. So no clarity was provided, which of course, just caused the situation to continue to worsen. This caused delays and, as a result, the organization lost a lot of money because, in the end, a third-party provider had to close out some of the deliverables ...

All this due to a lack of empathy—the CEO putting themselves in the shoes of the aggrieved and having compassion for their situation.

Space for humanity

It is, of course, very easy to beat up on leaders; they are easy targets. When was the last time you came across a media article that wasn't bashing leaders or cataloging how inept they are? We can ourselves easily get stuck in groupthink at the water cooler or on our coffee break and talk ill of our leaders. Some of that talk may be warranted, and some of it may be unwarranted or exaggerated, but it all contributes to a toxic workplace culture.

If we look dispassionately at what it takes to be successful as a leader, however, we must recognize that it is a hard and lonely job. If we are to move forward and repair our workplace culture so that all people can thrive, we need to address the unfair targeting of leaders, who don't all fit the mold of bad leadership. They may make some mistakes, but that doesn't necessarily mean that they are incompetent and uncaring. If we want to enjoy a workplace culture that supports psychological safety, it must benefit all people—including our leaders.

If we look dispassionately at what it takes to be successful as a leader, we must recognize that it is a hard and lonely job.

What is needed is space for humanity in the workplace, using empathy as a vehicle to bring it in. Ask yourself: 'When was the last time I empathized with a leader that I work with?'. You don't have to feel bad or sorry for them, because they are well compensated. On the other hand, you shouldn't assume that they are deliberately trying to make your life miserable.

Imagine for a moment your boss on their way to work, in their car or whatever means of transportation they take. How likely do you think it is that they are strategizing ways to ruin your day? That they are thinking, 'How can I make Linda's life or John's life more difficult today? How can I really piss them off?'. It is almost certain that they aren't; there is simply too much on their plate for them to be thinking like that. Is it likely that, by the time they get to work, they will have taken some decisions that impact you, making your day more difficult? Yes, it is. But that added difficulty is an unfortunate side-effect rather than an intentional strategy.

If we are to heal the workplace toxicity that currently exists globally, we have to make space for humanity; and the only way to do that is to have empathy for all people, not some people. If we limit our empathy to certain groups of people at work, it misses the point. Empathy is a right that all should have access to and benefit from.

If we are to heal the workplace toxicity that currently exists globally, we have to make space for humanity.

Modeling vulnerability

So how should leaders create a culture of empathy? One way of doing this is to show vulnerability, to say to your direct reports, 'Listen, how about you put yourself in my shoes. What would you do if you were me?'. This could land poorly. It could sound as if you are sidestepping your responsibility as a leader, which is to make decisions, and your direct reports might think, 'Hang on a minute. You're paid to make the decisions. Don't ask me to make them for you.'

Such an approach is more likely to succeed if you provide some context. We all know that leaders are making decisions with limited information and therefore sometimes get them wrong. You might therefore show a little contrition and say, 'Hey, I think I made a mistake on that decision last week, but with the limited information I had, that looked like the best decision at the time. If you were in my shoes, what would you have done?'.

Modeling vulnerability in this way is, of course, tricky; it requires both skill and psychological safety. But if a leader wants to create an environment within their team where there is two-way empathy, it can be the only way. Modeling vulnerability is like offering an olive branch, building a bridge that then becomes a platform for mutual communication and creates the transparency necessary for both parties to see what the other is going through. That is how their relationship can be strengthened and solidified.

Embracing polarities

'No one is always right and no one is always wrong' is another of those axioms whose origin is unknown. I heard it from acclaimed Canadian psychologist, author, and media commentator Jordan

Peterson, who was explaining that things are less black and white than they are gray. It is an idea that is generally foreign to politicians, who are hardwired to believe that they are always right and their opponents always wrong—the complete antithesis of what we have said in terms of the value of an opponent in pushing us to our limits.

If we simply shut out opposing viewpoints—like politicians and the former CEO of Company X—we are shutting down the conversation and no one benefits. We all simply become more ingrained and more entrenched, more rigidly contained inside our silos, incapable of taking things to the next level and transforming our workplaces. And if we aren't able to transform at that level, the organizations or the businesses that we work for will also suffer. There is a business bottom line impact, too.

So one of the challenges that we need to meet if we are going to be effective, not only in work but in life more broadly, is to make peace with polarities, to accept that two opposing views can both be true.

One of the challenges that we need to meet if we are going to be effective is to make peace with polarities.

As leaders, we may be in pole position to take a decision that impacts other people (and occasionally be on the receiving end of a decision that is beyond our control and has an impact on us), but we must also acknowledge that, however justified we feel a decision to be, if it impacts other people negatively, they have the right to feel aggrieved. The two things can be true. Part of our ability to evolve and level up our leadership is to embrace this concept.

In the last chapter I quoted John Stuart Mill, 'He who knows only his own side of the case, knows little of that ...', which also applies here. Having empathy is not about agreeing with the opposite viewpoint, but about at least suspending judgment long enough to digest it and see its merits. Only then will you be in a place of understanding where you can make an informed choice. You may go against it in the end, but you've at least let it in and appreciated its merits.

In an earlier chapter I referenced Joseph Campbell's *The Hero's Journey*, which shows us that we are all the heroes of our own story. This can, however, lead us into the fallacy of believing that we are always right and that the things we do can never negatively impact others, making it extremely difficult for us to look in the mirror and see the flaws in ourselves. Understanding also that no one is always right or wrong allows us to see that, as humans, we are flawed and should therefore act with some humility.

This understanding should ground us and make us true to ourselves. It should make us constantly review and reflect on our behavior and how it impacts others. It will make us vulnerable to moments of doubt, when we could be right or we could be wrong—but there is nothing wrong with that.

Allowing for organizational realities

A common complaint at the organizations I go into is: 'We're under-resourced.' What that really means is, 'We don't have the exact headcount that we would like' or 'We don't have the budget that we need to deliver on what is being asked of us.' Either (or both) of these things could be true, but the reality is that no one is ever working in ideal conditions. There are always competing interests, which constantly get in the way of the perfect outcome.

No one is ever working in ideal conditions. There are always competing interests, which constantly get in the way of the perfect outcome.

Some of this is within our control and some is not. Some is beyond the control of the organization itself. But there are often times when a decision has to be made as to what is possible and what is not possible. If we expand the headcount or increase the budget, what will be the knock-on effects? Will it be at the cost of people who deserve a pay raise, for example?

Thus, organizational realities will often guide or limit what is possible. But because leaders are the figureheads that are attached to the decision, they are, rightly or wrongly, held responsible for the emotional impact of what is decided (and sometimes even for the realities that necessitated the decision). We get stuck in the mindset that we 'deserve' or 'need' or 'want' things and lose sight of the wider ecosystem. We don't live in an independent world. We live in a very interconnected one, where decisions in one part of the world, geopolitically, can impact the value of currencies in others. Inside an organization, decisions at one end of the business will impact decisions that need to be taken at the other end. Nothing works in isolation. We must always be mindful of that.

Not everything is personal

We must also not fall into the trap of thinking, like the former CEO of Company X, that things are personal. If a decision was taken by a leader that impacts us, but we are not able to access the context of why that decision was made, we may see that decision as a personal attack. Not everything is personal; not everyone is out to get you. But it can feel that way if we don't allow ourselves enough time to reflect and recenter, focusing on the things that matter.

If we get stuck in our feelings and get mad at our line manager or at the organization, if we give up hope that things are going to change without seeking employment elsewhere, we are allowing learned helplessness to take hold.

If you see your leader as 'the enemy', the relational energy between you and that leader is going to be antagonistic. In your head, you are the hero of your story and that leader who took a decision that impacted you is the villain—not the dragon you need to slay, but an unconquerable antagonist—and you are the victim. If you remain in a condition where you see yourself as a victim, how is that going to help you move forward in your career, in life?

You are disempowering yourself. Even if the organization is transforming, even if the culture is improving, you are not in a position to experience the positive change that is happening around you, because you have allowed yourself to become entrenched in a silo.

By staying in the mindset that we have been victimized or aggrieved, that we have been hurt, we are never going to be able to move on because we cannot heal. We are choosing to remain wounded.

We need to look at every situation as an opportunity to grow.

Instead, we need to look at every situation as an opportunity to grow. As we have seen, opponents are necessary—to push us to our limits—so we should regard them as welcome antagonists, not unhelpful enemies. Every situation that frustrates us is giving us information that can help us to grow provided we stay true to ourselves as opposed to becoming combative. As Joseph Campbell's *Hero's Journey* shows us, every challenge presents an opportunity to demonstrate who we are.

What often happens is that in the heat of the moment we lose sight of the things that identify who we are; we lose our sense of self. But that is the defining moment for us to show how strongly committed we are to the things that matter: to dignity, integrity, respect, and empathy. If in that moment we drop the ball, can we really say that we have high ethical standards, that we are of good character and competence? Can we say that we handled the situation well if we immediately abandon the things that are important to us? Of course, when we have an emotional response, when our nervous system is activated, it takes time for us to regulate and repair. So we must take the time for that to happen.

The obstacle is the way

The title of Ryan Holiday's 2015 book *The Obstacle is the Way*[19] comes from the *Meditations* of Marcus Aurelius, which the stoic emperor wrote in the second century: 'The mind adapts and converts to its own purposes the obstacle to our acting. The impediment to action advances action. What stands in the way becomes the way.'

In other words, because nothing goes to plan, we should plan to adjust to circumstances. The things that go wrong are part of the way forward. Whether we are forecasting budgets or making strategic plans, we know that, once they go live, we will need to make adjustments—to adapt, improvise, and overcome. The adversity that disrupts our plan or our goal becomes part of the thing that we need to overcome. We must embrace it, use it as an opportunity to persist and succeed, despite obstacles. We must allow ourselves to see adversity as a way of leveraging all of our resources.

---

19 Profile Books (2015).

> *Because nothing goes to plan, we should plan to adjust to circumstances.*

There is a connection here with the concept of eustress that we discussed in Chapter 2. It is no use our complaining that the market isn't working with us, or that we have just lost 30% of the budget we thought we were going to have on a certain project. There is an opportunity here to become more creative, to still deliver on the project despite that 30% budget cut. And the sensation we will get from achieving that goal is exponentially more beneficial to us than if we'd had the full budget and delivered as originally planned.

Your respect for yourself widens when you go through trials and tribulations.

> *Your respect for yourself widens when you go through trials and tribulations.*

RIDE or DIE

We have now looked at the four pillars of informed leadership: respect, integrity, dignity, and empathy. Together they form the acronym RIDE, the implication being that, if you ensure that they are all firmly in place, you will have a smooth ride through life.

The 'opposite' of this is to DIE, which stands for deceitful, inhumane, and egocentric: having no respect for others but deliberately deceiving or misleading them, lacking compassion and empathy for others, and thinking only of oneself without regard for the feeling or desires of others.

These acronyms are, of course, rather glib, but they may serve to remind us of the essential principles of informed leadership: It is a set of values, a mindset, a commitment. You are opting in.

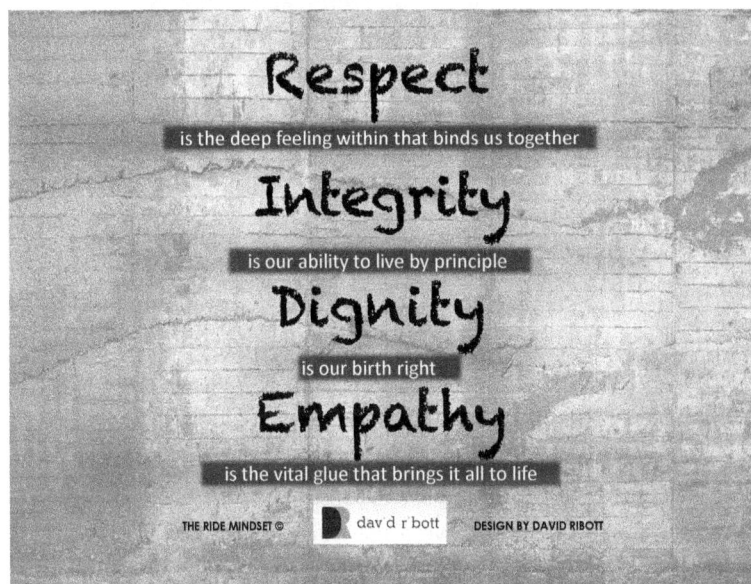

Informed leadership is a set of values, a mindset, a commitment. You are opting in.

In the final part of this book we will define the profile of an informed leader: the qualities required of them and how they can use those qualities—and the RIDE mindset—to align purpose, boost performance, and achieve prosperity.

Summary

Empathy means sharing someone else's feelings or experiences by putting yourself in that person's situation. With empathy comes compassion, coming to others without judgment.

Leaders, too, deserve our empathy; they aren't deliberately trying to ruin your life. In the workplace, we have to make space for humanity, which means showing vulnerability and acting with humility.

We must be at peace with polarities. Unless we accept that no one is always right and no one is always wrong, we will become more entrenched inside our silos and less able to transform our workplaces. Having empathy doesn't mean agreeing with the opposite viewpoint, but at least suspending judgment long enough to digest it and see its merits.

We must also recognize that we are never working in ideal conditions. Organizational realities will always get in the way. And in our increasingly interconnected world, we can have no control over the factors that impact our organization.

Not everything is personal, and not everyone is out to get you, even though it can feel that way sometimes. Every situation is an opportunity to grow, and we must never lose sight of the things we are committed to: dignity, integrity, respect, and empathy.

Since nothing goes to plan, we must plan to adjust to circumstances, to use obstacles as stepping stones, to embrace them, to use them as opportunities to succeed. In short, we must RIDE or DIE. If we aren't oriented to an operating system where respect, integrity, dignity, and empathy are central, we will fail to be effective leaders—to be evolved people. We will be governed by our emotional responses without the regulation that is needed to make sense of things and successfully navigate our way through the day.

PART THREE

Informed Leadership In Action

In this final part of the book, we build on the foundation of informed leadership and look at what a leader can achieve when they have a solid RIDE mindset in place. We look first at the essential qualities of an informed leader—the ABCs—and see that the two things, leadership mindset and leadership qualities, go hand in hand; that, while a leader could be effective with just the ABCs of informed leadership, they may struggle if the foundation is not firmly in place, or at least being worked on to get it solidified. They may not entirely fall apart, but they will probably achieve only marginal success as leaders.

We then return to the three Ps of informed leadership we discussed in Chapter 1—purpose, performance, and prosperity—to see how the combination of a solid foundation, the essential qualities of informed leadership, and a sharp focus on the three Ps will enable a leader to achieve success.

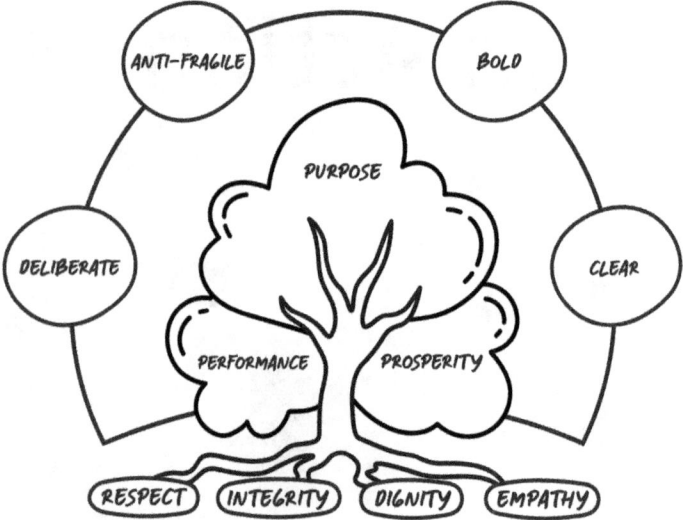

7

The ABCs of Informed Leaders

What are the key qualities a leader needs to have in order to be effective? I believe that there are four of them: An effective leader must be anti-fragile, bold, clear, and deliberate. Notice that I say 'effective'. Having these qualities will not necessarily make a leader perfect, but it will mean that they can be effective.

In previous chapters I have referred to learned helplessness—a state that can all too easily pervade an organization if its leadership has no clear system of accountability. 'Why should I bother to make an effort in the interest of the organization when I am getting a 5 out of 5 in my performance appraisals anyway?'.

I am reminded of the movie *One Flew Over The Cuckoo's Nest*, in which Randle McMurphy (Jack Nicholson) plays a petty criminal who is sent to a state mental institution for 'rehabilitation' and is shocked to discover that other inmates are there by choice, that they are happier to be helpless than to take responsibility for their own wellbeing and success in life. As one of them says, 'Nobody complains about all the fog. Bad as it is, you can slip back in it and feel safe. That's what McMurphy can't understand, us wanting to be safe. He keeps trying to drag us out of the fog, out in the open where we'd be easy to get at.'

When we look at the former CEO of Company X, we see not only that their style of leadership was exactly the kind that leads to an organizational culture of learned helplessness—of giving up, of disengaging—but also that, just as in the movie all the inmates love to hate Nurse Ratched, who dishes out their daily medication and controls their every waking moment, so the employees of Company X come to despise their CEO while at the same time being dependent on them. Yet they remain where they are, on the basis that the devil you know is better than the devil you don't know.

Looking at the role of the CEO from the other side of the desk, however, we must recognize that being a leader is no simple task. We may be qualified for it from a technical point of view, but do we have the qualities we need to perform it effectively?

It is important to understand that being a leader is a process rather than an ability or capability. A leader must continuously learn and evolve. There is no absolute solution to all their problems. Their 'operating system' needs to be continually upgraded.

Being a leader is a process rather than an ability or capability. A leader must continuously learn and evolve.

Let us look at each of the elements of this operating system in turn.

Anti-fragile

So often in organizations we hear talk about the importance of being agile, of being responsive to the volatility, uncertainty, complexity, and ambiguity of the modern business world. Agility is great, but in order to level up and be really effective, we need something stronger, because agility is a bit like a rubber band. The more you pull at it, the more it will lose its elasticity and stretch, and the more likely it is eventually to break. In that sense, agility is fragility.

What we need to become, in fact, is anti-fragile, as defined by Nassim Taleb in his book *Antifragile: Things that Gain from Disorder*.[20] This means having the ability to bend but not break, learning how to take a punch, to be like a great tree whose branches are swayed by the wind but that remains rooted to the spot.

Your solidity is due to the firmness of your foundation: respect, integrity, dignity, and empathy. These are what keep you grounded amid the storms and stresses of life.

Bold

Often when we recognize entrepreneurs or innovators, such as Steve Jobs, for the things that they have achieved, we acknowledge that it is because they have been bold. Purely in

---

20 Penguin (2013).

terms of functionality, there may be little to choose between an iPhone and a Samsung, but Jobs saw beyond mere functionality and was able to develop products that created a cult-like following. There is something about owning an iPhone that gives people a sense of community—which is due to Apple's boldness in their approach to product design.

In any organization, it is often easier to play safe. It is more predictable and therefore more comfortable. Being bold requires taking a leap of faith, which often causes resistance.

The CEO of a business is often required to push back against the Board—and the Board can be tough. The former CEO of Company X never pushed back; they just said yes to everything. Which meant that they were not really a leader, but rather a project manager, conducting work streams, delegating what had been assigned to them downstream to their teams but not owning anything. Similarly, when the CEO's C-suite team, their top 20 people, came to them with things that they needed, the CEO wouldn't be bold enough to ask the board for those things.

As leaders, we cannot afford merely to play safe; playing safe doesn't move the needle. It can even take you out of the picture altogether and make your organization redundant.

As leaders, we cannot afford merely to play safe; playing safe doesn't move the needle.

If we look at the list of the world's top 100 companies, it remained pretty stable for most of the second half of the 20th century. Since then, however, the list has been constantly changing, and it is likely that the majority of the top 100 companies of 2050 don't even exist today. If organizations aren't bold, they are very unlikely to have the competitive advantage they need to survive; and since organizations don't exist without leaders to steer them and empower their people, those leaders must themselves be bold. Like Jobs and Apple, they must create a following, a sense of belonging, a workplace culture that people want to be a part of.

Clear

It may be stating the obvious, but to be clear is paramount. Without clarity, no one knows what is expected of them, what they can and can't do. As we have seen, without clear KPIs and a clear system of accountability, they will not commit to a task, a team, or the organization as a whole.

When you are clear, you are committing to something; there is a frame of reference; everyone can see what the original intention was, what needs to be done to achieve it, and—afterwards—whether what needed to be done has actually been done. When the original intention hasn't been clearly articulated, all those things become difficult.

In the military, to overcome this obstacle there is a phenomenon known as commander's intent, which in simple terms allows leaders on the ground in battlefields to improvise as necessary and with confidence within the stated objectives because they had clarity on the direction and ultimate goal of the operation.

One of the first things the new CEO of Company X did was register KPIs in the system so that everyone understood what their role was and what was expected of them. Even if they didn't always agree with those KPIs because they thought they were too ambitious or, dare I say, bold, and even if they subsequently had to adapt those expectations in light of changing circumstances, they were better prepared because they had a sense of what success looked like and there was an identifiable marker that was clearly articulated and that they could commit to and get behind.

Deliberate

Many studies have been undertaken into peak performance—in sport, in music, in other areas—and 'the 10,000-hour rule' is well known. In their book *Peak: Secrets from the New Science of Expertise*,[21] Anders Ericsson and Robert Pool go beyond this idea to investigate the nature of the practice that peak performers must undertake and concludes that for practice to be effective it must be deliberate. Too often we get distracted by other things, which may be connected to the thing we want to achieve but are not the thing itself. We find ourselves thinking about the thing, dreaming about achieving it, but thinking or dreaming about it isn't doing it. To actually achieve what you want to achieve, you must do the thing; and the only way to get better at doing it is to be deliberate.

> *To actually achieve what you want to achieve, you must do the thing; and the only way to get better at doing it is to be deliberate.*

If you are training to be a commercial pilot and learning how to define and follow a flight plan, you cannot be haphazard about your practice. Being off by even a couple of degrees in your flight plan can make the difference between landing in New York City or in Toronto.

You cannot, from one day to the next, get better at something without deliberately practicing the things that will

---

21   Houghton Mifflin Harcourt (2016).

get you better. There are very specific activities and exercises that need to be done in order to make that happen; and those actions or activities need to align with the desired outcome.

The 20/60/20 rule

At this point in the book you may be wondering whether the juice is worth the squeeze: 'Why bother with all this—being anti-fragile, bold, clear, and deliberate—when I can get by without it, when the effort probably won't be worth it anyway?'. The answer to that question is that, if you don't make the effort to be anti-fragile, bold, clear, and deliberate, you are vulnerable to corruption.

Corruption doesn't only mean blackmailing people and taking bribes; it also means influencing people to make decisions that are in your interest rather than the wider interest. Surprisingly, the majority of people are susceptible to such influence. In his book *Corruptible: Who Gets Power and How It Changes Us*,[22] Brian Klaas introduces us to his 20/60/20 model, according to which 20% of people will always act in an ethical manner, 20% of people will always act in a corrupt manner—to a greater or lesser extent—and the 60% of people in between are open to being influenced: by bad leadership, by negative peer pressure, by toxic (social) media campaigns …

In Chapter 4 we saw how Jeffrey Skilling, an initially honest and upright person, turned out to be one of the biggest fraudsters in history. Because he was vulnerable to corruption. Because he was operating in an environment where there was no strong ethical foundation, no clear definitions of what was right and what was wrong.

---

22   John Murray (2022).

So the question that matters is not, 'Why should I bother?', but 'What cost am I willing to bear?'. Would you rather do the work, or would you rather allow yourself to be vulnerable to corruption? The choice is yours, but let it be a choice you can live with, not one that you will end up regretting later.

Effective

If we put the first four ABCs—anti-fragile, bold, clear, and deliberate—together, we are putting ourselves in the best possible position to be effective, the fifth of the ABCs. But we need to put them *all* together; if any of these elements is missing, you will not have the qualities necessary to be an effective leader. If you are anti-fragile but not deliberate, you may occasionally be effective; if you are anti-fragile and clear but not bold, you are probably just going to continue to hit your baseline numbers and not achieve anything more; if you are clear and deliberate but not anti-fragile or bold, you are just as unlikely to move the needle.

If, on the other hand, we are able to bend but not break, there is no situation that we can't handle. If we are bold, we will remain fearless in the face of fire. If we can then set clarity around the target, around the goals we want to achieve and also hold accountability along the way, and be deliberate about the activities that we need to focus on in order to achieve those outcomes, then we are sure to be effective.

In talking about being effective, I am not referring to the classic modus operandi of effectiveness: doing whatever it takes to increase the bottom line. We are talking here about effectiveness in terms of aligned purpose, greater performance, and increased prosperity. About benefiting the organization not just financially, but holistically.

As we have seen, the former CEO of Company X may have been anti-fragile and bold, but they were neither clear nor deliberate, which made them ineffective. Whatever they might have achieved in P&L terms, the organization's toxic culture, the staff's silo mentality, their learned helplessness all remained ingrained and ultimately destructive.

With a new CEO who has all the required qualities, as well as a solid foundation in terms of the RIDE mindset, the mood at Company X is very different—although it is still early days. Gone are the anxiousness and anxiety of not knowing what to do and throwing things against the wall to see what sticks. In their place is a mood of challenging the old ways of doing things to unlock the hidden potential of the organization and of its people, a sense of direction for both today and the future with no guarantee of success, but a confidence that the captain now sailing the ship is the right person at the helm.

Let me be clear: Being effective doesn't mean that you aren't ever going to make mistakes; it doesn't mean that you will never be wrong or make a bad decision. What it does mean is that you are in a position to tackle the big challenges that your organization is going to face. It doesn't ensure that you will always be successful, but you will have at least a fighting chance of overcoming them because your responsiveness and resiliency to recover from a deficit are enhanced.

Working with clients across North America, Europe, the Middle East and Africa, and Asia-Pacific regions, I have come to realize that those challenges are best overcome by leaders that have a RIDE mindset and the ABCs of informed leadership. They are the ones who most successfully lead their organizations toward their purpose, improve their performance, and achieve prosperity for everyone connected with them—including themselves.

In the final three chapters we will see how they do so.

Summary

A leader needs four key qualities in order to be effective: They must be anti-fragile, bold, clear, and deliberate. Being anti-fragile means bending without breaking; being bold means taking a leap of faith rather than playing safe; being clear means making sure everyone knows what is expected of them; being deliberate means constantly practicing what you have to do.

If you don't make the effort to be anti-fragile, bold, clear, and deliberate, you are vulnerable to situations where your static skillset leaves you out of your depth and corruptible behavior, whether conscious or unconscious, becomes a more likely outcome. With all those qualities in place you are sure to be an effective leader. This doesn't mean that you will never make mistakes, that you will never be wrong or make a bad decision; it means that you are in a position to tackle the big challenges that your organization is going to face.

Leadership is a process rather than an ability or a capability—a continuous process of learning and evolving.

8
Purpose

In Chapter 1 we saw that there is often a misalignment between an organization's purpose and function—what is sometimes called mission creep. In many cases, leaders unconsciously reinforce this misalignment, unaware that there is a disconnect between what they believe and say their purpose is and their actual behavior and actions. This mismatch has been explained by Chris Argyris[23] in his distinction between 'espoused theories' and 'theories in use', whereby organizations, teams, and individuals tend to claim that they operate according to a particular set of theories or principles (which they would like to be the case) but actually follow a different set of concepts or priorities.

---

23 e.g. *Organizational Traps: Leadership, Culture, Organizational Design* (Oxford, 2010); *Integrating the Individual and the Organization* (John Wiley and Sons, Inc., 1964); *On Organizational Learning* (Blackwell Publishers, 1999).

Ideally, the two should harmonize to create synergy, but what often happens is that they clash or collide, which can create a combustible situation, depending on the amount of friction between beliefs and behavior.

Because this is largely unconscious behavior, when challenged, we (our ego) typically resist(s) admitting to the disjunction. As David Fraser explains, 'Unaddressed, ego will maintain the discrepancy between espoused theories and theories in use, preventing the organization (or the person) from really understanding itself, in turn preventing it from adapting and changing and growing. An important role of leaders is to overcome this tendency, both in themselves and in others.'[24]

It starts with you

If you don't have a purpose for yourself, it is going to be extremely difficult to align your purpose with your organization's purpose—which brings us back to the question of self-awareness we discussed in Chapter 2. If we want to improve our effectiveness as leaders, we must first look in the mirror and make ourselves aware of how we are behaving as leaders. This takes fearless honesty.

The foundation is you, so you must look inside yourself before you look at others. Ask yourself, 'What is my contribution to this situation? What could I do differently?'. If we don't have the capacity to look at ourselves, we are only ever going to see half the picture.

---

24 David Fraser, "What's the Difference Between Espoused Theories and Theories in Use?", *DF/Dr David Fraser*, 20 March 2015, https://drdavidfraser.com/2015/03/20/whats-the-difference-between-espoused-theories-and-theories-in-use/ (accessed 27 March, 2025).

Look inside yourself before you look at others.

An important part of my work with senior leaders is 'shadowing'. You can only see so much in a coaching or consulting session; to be able to see the true character and capacity of a leader, you need to spend time with them throughout the day, because after a certain point they will be unable to put on an act anymore; the flow and the pace of the day will take over sooner or later, and their naturalness, their authenticity will start to show. No one can pretend all day. So imagine you have someone shadowing you all day long, and you will begin to see your true self.

This self-reflection must go beyond simplistic, black-and-white definitions of 'types' of leader. There is much talk, for example, about 'male' vs. 'female' leadership and 'passive' vs. 'active' leadership. To argue that one is better than the other is to miss the point. What is needed is to combine the different aspects of our leadership persona: to integrate our 'shadow', to use Jung's term. As long as you reject a part of you, you are rejecting all of you.

As long as you reject a part of you, you are rejecting all of you.

The same applies to organizations. An organization's stated purpose, in terms of its mission statement, its vision, and its values, is an identified marker of what it believes in. It says to its employees, and potential employees, 'This is who we are; this is what we stand for.' It is an important way to build a sense of belonging, of connection, of commitment, a sense of tribe. An employee might decide to work at a particular organization because its purpose speaks to them, because there is common ground between what they believe and what it *states* it believes. If, however, after being onboarded, getting past probation, and working there for a while, they see or get the sense that their leadership is behaving in a way that misaligns with that purpose, this will cause friction and can seriously disrupt their ability to be productive and to remain a fully committed and engaged employee to the best of their capacity. They will think, 'If leadership doesn't care about the purpose, why should I?'. This is not to say that they, as individual employees, are lacking professional ethics. It is simply that when an organization's purpose is misaligned with its behavior, it becomes extremely difficult for its employees—no matter how strong they are, no matter how self-evolved as professionals—to coexist in that ecosystem. At the end of the day, they are only human. They will disengage.

People disengage because engagement hurts. It is a defense mechanism, designed to protect them. They will retreat into themselves, put on a mask, and say, 'I don't care. This is just a job. I'll just clock in and clock out.'

People disengage because engagement hurts.

Of course, an organization must do what it can to remain competitive in the marketplace; it must change as the marketplace changes. And those changes will inevitably sometimes create a lag between purpose and function, between espoused theory and theory in use. But any such lag must be acknowledged and, as leaders, we must commit to doing something about it. To allow it to remain a lag is to allow interference in your operating system to persist—as if you ignored a glitch in your computer, hoping it would go away, rather than finding out what was wrong with it and getting it repaired, until one day the hard drive crashes and you lose everything you have been working on.

It is therefore clear that, if an organization is to be effective (successful), it must be an integrated whole, with a single, aligned purpose; and it is up to its leader(s) to ensure that this is the reality. Yet, in my conversations with leaders, the concept of purpose is seldom even brought up. It is the elephant in the room, which is simply overlooked.

Again, purpose alignment begins with you, as a leader. If the senior leadership in an organization is not committed to its purpose, it will be very difficult for them to figure out how to align its workforce with the organization's needs. If we aren't benchmarking our direct reports' performance against that purpose, how are we measuring it? If we aren't responding to market conditions and optimizing and activating our workforce in parallel with the identified priorities of the organization in order for it to sustain success, how can we expect them to do what is needed?

You need to know what you are aiming at and where you are starting from to understand how far away you are.

You need to know what you are aiming at and where you are starting from to understand how far away you are.

Long-term vs. short-term goals

Meetings at any strategic level that don't align to the purpose and only look at what is needed in terms of KPIs are missing the point, because what they are saying indirectly to the workforce is that the organization's purpose, its long-term aspiration, doesn't really matter. All that matters is short-term wins over the course of a year or a quarter. After a while, it becomes a difficult habit to unfossilize.

Yes, any organization has targets, which may be total revenue or profit or EBITDA, or may be a net gain year on year or an increase in market share, but those too must be aligned with its purpose.

Like many organizations, Company X had experienced challenges during Covid and, coming out of the pandemic, had received direction from its board that it needed to be more aggressive in order to increase commercial targets and overall sales. That push was then thrust upon the management team, which suddenly had to achieve targets that were 40% or 50% higher than their best years ever and was expected to turn the organization's fortunes around in just one year.

That wasn't in itself a bad thing. The problem was that the then CEO didn't set a strategy that showed how the organization would get there. Everything was ad hoc, and they threw ideas at things that contradicted the organization's stated purpose. One of the CEO's direct reports, at C-suite level, voiced their concern: 'Hey, how does this align to our purpose? How can we align long-term vision, long-term aspirations with short-term goals that build toward that?'. But they were merely chided: 'We don't have time to align to the purpose. We have hard targets that need to be met this year.' It was as if the CEO had said, 'At this moment, purpose doesn't matter. It's all about profit.'

Whether or not the former CEO was conscious of this at the time, the knock-on effect of the behavior of staff came to look like a scene from *The Hunger Games*. Decorum went out the window and different teams within the organization that were meant to work cross-functionally simply ran over anyone that got in their way in a desperate bid to meet those ambitious targets.

They did hit their numbers, but the damage that was done in terms of organizational culture and ethics, stakeholder, client, and customer relations, and brand reputation was incalculable.

All because the CEO of Company X had sidestepped its purpose in order to achieve short-term targets.

A real-world example of a similar situation is the merger of Boeing with McDonnell Douglas in 1996. Until then, Boeing had been committed to engineering excellence and a safety-first culture—a purpose that led to a reputation for quality and reliability. In contrast, McDonnell Douglas, which had undertaken a series of unsuccessful ventures, was focused on cost-reduction, market competitiveness, and shareholder value. Its stated purpose was 'good enough for government'.

After the merger, these very different values influenced Boeing's business decisions and strategy. Development of the 737 Max, in particular, failed to meet overambitious deadlines, exceeded unrealistic budgets, and ultimately led to among the most catastrophic events in Boeing's more than century-long history: two crashes, in 2018 and 2019, of the new plane that resulted in the deaths of 346 people, which were found to have been due to the malfunctioning of a new software system.

Where you get to vs. how you get there

These examples highlight the fact that the really important question is not 'Where do you want to get to?' but 'How are you going to get there?'. While the first question can be answered by quantitative data, the second requires a qualitative analysis. It is all very well achieving financial targets, but if we break everything along the way like a bull in a china shop, what are you left with?

> The really important question is not 'Where do you want to get to?' but 'How are you going to get there?'.

There are times, you will say, when such an approach is necessary, when the very survival of the organization is at stake. Admittedly. But what is required in such cases is honesty and transparency, which are born of integrity and respect: a statement such as, 'At this moment, in order for us to survive as an entity in the retail space, this is what we have to do, and we need all hands on deck in order to achieve it. It's a short-term approach—we're looking at six to eight months—that will determine whether we can get the company out of the red.' Integrity demands and respect dictates that you explain, contextualize, rationalize, and justify the decision to your people.

Moving forward with an absence of communication creates a vacuum, which leaves your workforce having to interpret, to infer, to guess what is happening and why and what is expected of them. Without that knowledge, they will justifiably look at the organization's purpose and at the actions and the behaviors of its leaders and see a misalignment.

If you don't communicate directly, you are communicating indirectly, which is far less clear.

If you don't communicate directly, you are communicating indirectly, which is far less clear.

Sense of team

Clear communication and common commitment to a single purpose create a sense of team—a sense that must start at the top and cascade down through the organization. If members of the C-suite—who might number anything between five and twelve—have no sense of team, how can they be expected to create a sense of team among their direct reports and the rest of their staff?

Imagine a marriage in which the two partners have different aims and different priorities. How long is it likely to last? And what will it feel like for the people involved in it while it does? They will be wondering, 'What are we trying to do here? Where are we headed and why?'.

If a marriage isn't working, of course, you can get a divorce. In a senior management team within an organization, on the other hand, you can't get 'divorced' from your 'partners' (unless you leave the organization altogether). But if they have different aims and priorities, there will be no sense of team. You will end up with what we have talked about before: a silo mentality, with verticals shoring themselves up and not wanting to cooperate or collaborate with one another.

Then, if there is no sense of team among the senior leaders in your organization, that absence will cascade down and lead to dysfunction, chaos, and the human response of disengagement. So the question becomes: Do we want to cultivate a sense of team? If we do, then we need to be aligned. We need to do our due diligence, to check and confirm that we, as the senior management team, are aligned to purpose, and cascading down that sense of alignment, that sense of team.

It may happen accidentally but, if so, it isn't by design; and if it isn't by design, it is beyond your control. Purpose must be by design. The time and effort it takes to cultivate purpose as a statement to land on is detailed and deliberate. An organization's purpose is meant to evoke some sort of emotional response, something that inspires. It can't be left to chance, because in that case you don't know what response you are going to get.

Purpose must be by design. The time and effort it takes to cultivate purpose as a statement to land on is detailed and deliberate.

Modeling alignment to purpose

When the new CEO arrived at Company X, there was a recommitment to the basics, starting with purpose and diving into what it meant to bring this purpose to life, what behaviors and values were needed among the workforce—including the company's leaders—to achieve that.

They looked at the company's stated purpose and then at the way it functioned and saw that they were misaligned. The CEO said, 'Look, we've drifted. I'm not sure why, but we're going to get back to being a purpose-led organization where our decisions and actions are going to be in alignment with its stated purpose, where we are going to embody the behaviors and the values that emanate from it.'

With that simple statement came a calming of the chaos, a sense of safety and hope for the future. There followed a healing process, during which the damage that had been done by the mission creep under the regime of the former CEO was gradually repaired and the toxic workplace culture made healthy again.

It was as if the organization had been experiencing heavy weather in a storm and the sun had come out again. There was enough safety in the system for everyone to want to be part of it again and feel that they belonged.

As a leader, you can effect that kind of transformation by reminding your people why the organization exists, because why it exists is directly connected to its purpose.

Summary

If you don't have a purpose for yourself, it will be difficult to align your purpose with your organization's purpose. So if we want to improve our effectiveness as leaders, we must first make ourselves aware of how we are behaving as leaders. The same applies to organizations whose mission statement is a marker of what they believe in. If an organization is to be effective, it must be an integrated whole, with a single, aligned purpose; and it is up to its leaders to ensure that this is the reality.

It is not so much a matter of getting where you want to get to but getting there in the right way. Creating a sense of team requires clear communication and common commitment to a single purpose, which must start at the top and cascade down through the organization.

Alignment must be by design, as must purpose, which should evoke an emotional response. Its cultivation must therefore be detailed and deliberate; it cannot be left to chance.

9

Performance

When it comes to performance, we have seen the importance of clarity, of clearly communicating what is required of a direct report, so that they know what they need to do to achieve a 5 out of 5, what 'success' actually looks like. What is also required is to give direct reports appropriate latitude to do their job within the scope of their remit and to be tolerant, within reason, of any mistakes they may make. To improve their performance we then need to put our direct reports in challenging situations. We need to go beyond meeting KPIs and ensure cross-functional collaboration. We need to measure everything we want to manage, and we need to consider not just productivity but people.

Let us look at each of these requirements in turn.

Latitude and tolerance

As we know, nothing goes according to plan—or, as the saying goes, 'We plan, God laughs.' As leaders we therefore need not only to have the capacity to adapt, improvise, and overcome, but also to give our direct reports the latitude to do the same, to make their own (informed) decisions 'on the fly' rather than constantly have to refer back to us for authorization, which not only delays action but also puts undue pressure on us and undermines their authority.

Hand in hand with giving latitude goes tolerating a reasonable level of mistakes. If we let someone make their own decisions, they will inevitably make mistakes (as would we if we made those decisions for them). We therefore need to 'allow' that. We must accept that 80% of their decisions will work and 20% won't and not condemn or shame them for the 20% that didn't, but rather praise them for their courage and initiative in making 80% good decisions while seeking to strengthen their accuracy over time. Otherwise, we will be succumbing to a blame culture and a silo mentality—which, as we have seen (in Chapter 3), we want to strenuously avoid—and our direct reports will not be bold but over-cautious; they will always 'play safe' and, as we have also seen on page 65, no amount of playing safe will lead to innovation or competitive advantage.

We do, of course, have to address the 20% of mistakes, but in a constructive way. We need to say something like, 'Yeah, you made a mistake here; you might have done this instead. But, given the unforeseen circumstances and consequent lack of clarity, and that you were working under less-than-ideal conditions, you did the best you could and you will be better prepared the next time something like this happens.'

In fact, the experience of failure and 'hardship' in this sense is necessary for our development and growth as leaders and also as people.

The experience of failure and 'hardship' in this sense is necessary for our development and growth as leaders and also as people.

Applying the 70-20-10 rule

The 70-20-10 rule (also referred to as a 'framework' and a 'model') is a leadership guideline developed by the Center for Creative Leadership.[25] It states that three types of experience, in a specific combination, are required for leadership growth: 70% of challenging assignments, 20% of developmental relationships, and 10% of training and study. The heavy weighting given in this equation to 'challenging assignments' shows the great importance of these in leadership development. In other words, we cannot become effective leaders simply by studying or being shown how to be leaders; we must put ourselves in situations that will test us to the limit—and sometimes make us fail. Given that our direct reports are also leaders of others, we must give them the same exposure to such challenges.

As I have said before, we hear a lot about post-traumatic stress (distress) but relatively little about post-traumatic growth (eustress). Even a disastrous or tragic experience can transform us, give us clarity and confidence or the inner resources to evolve and grow above the level at which we were previously operating. It can convert the 'trauma' of the experience into fuel that can propel us forward in ways we might not have imagined possible.

Even a disastrous or tragic experience can give us clarity and confidence or the inner resources to evolve and grow above the level at which we were previously operating.

25   See https://www.ccl.org/, accessed March 27, 2025.

We should therefore neither expect nor even want our direct reports to be 100% successful. Failure is hardship, which is the experience we need to grow, to better navigate the VUCA (volatility, uncertainty, complexity, and ambiguity) situations we will inevitably encounter in the future—because, like it or not, VUCA is the new normal; it is not going to go away.

Going back to what we saw in Chapter 1 with reference to falling leadership confidence levels: You can only have confidence in people if you know they are able to navigate tough terrains.

Beyond KPIs

Leaders are often focused on KPIs, which are, of course, important; but achieving KPIs is not the same as managing performance. Sometimes they meet in the middle, but not always.

KPIs are (desired) outcomes of a particular work stream or vertical or part of the business. They are essentially a measure of what work is done, while performance management is about how work is done. Looking only at KPIs gives us only a transactional view of performance, without being mindful of employee engagement (which is key to quality of performance) in that transaction. It is a one-dimensional, black-and-white measure that asks simply: Did we achieve the target, yes or no?

A more rounded and mature way of managing performance is to say, 'Okay, you hit your targets, but how did you get there? Did it come at the expense of cross-functional relationships with key internal stakeholders?'. Or, 'Okay, you didn't hit your targets, but why was that? Was it because there were so many insurmountable obstacles along the way?'.

It is vital to ask such questions, because the more data we have, the better understanding we will have of what is interfering with performance (see discussion of Tim Gallway's (P = P – I) Performance = Potential – Interference model on page 67).

The more data we have, the better understanding we will have of what is interfering with performance.

Cross-functional collaboration

School and university largely prepare us to work alone. Testing is individual and our gradings are not shared. We are brought up and developed within the academic track to stand on our own two feet. But when we exit university and take our first job, even if this is as an individual contributor, we are always part of a team. We are sharing pieces of a scope of work or a work stream among a group of three or four or five people. We are never truly working alone. Everything is integrated and requires some level of collaboration—which may be why we find collaboration challenging.

Everything is integrated and requires some level of collaboration—which may be why we find collaboration challenging.

It isn't so hard when we are working within a single team with one leader, for whom everyone on that team is a direct report. It gets more complicated when the work is cross-functional. Some organizations have figured out how to do this and some haven't. It is a question of design. Today, many organizations strive to be 'lean' and 'agile' and 'nimble' when in fact what they need to be is cross-functional, because no piece of business works on its own. Everything works cross-functionally.

Recognizing that, you would assume that organizations would have a mature process around shared KPIs, a weighting system that clearly shows what share of a KPI each vertical has: For example, HR has 50% of the responsibility for this KPI, finance has 25%, and facilities management has the other 25%. Yet when I go into an organization and ask those responsible for strategy and performance, 'How have you addressed shared KPIs?' I invariably get the answer, 'We're working on it.'

Most organizations don't address the issue because it is hard to do so. Under its former CEO Company X had been talking about implementing a shared KPI model for two years, but it was never initiated; a task force was never deployed to come up with a design.

It is hard for two reasons. First, because you have to get clear on which function should carry the front load of a particular performance outcome and which should play a supportive role. Second, because that weighting needs to be captured somehow by a quantitative metric.

The fact that it is hard, however, is not a reason not to do it. We must accept that the weighting will always be approximate, that we will never get it exactly right. It isn't a perfect world. But having such a system of shared KPIs in place will reduce a lot of tension in cross-functional work and mitigate the challenges inherent in developing good conflict management skills, which, as we know, is the most difficult competency for leaders to develop. Each team will know where it stands and what its responsibility is—who owns what.

Imagine a soccer team (football for everyone else outside the US) in which no field positions have been allocated, so that the players have no idea who should be defending or who should be attacking. How would that work? Even if each player is a star performer, they won't be able to work together effectively. The team is not set up for success. The same applies to an organization.

Measuring and managing

'What gets measured gets managed' is a popular phrase attributed to management guru Peter Drucker. It means that, to manage anything, you must know how it works; you must have information on it, data.

I can't tell you the number of times I have gone into an organization for one reason or another and we have started talking about performance and about the challenges that are being experienced in the business, which are often people issues, and I have said, 'Okay, so what data are you collecting on these issues? What data collection system are you using? Are you, for example, using Gallup's Q12 Employment Engagement Survey? Are you using McKinsey's Organizational Health Index? Are you using Great Place to Work[26] methodology?' and the answer has invariably been 'No.' Which tells me that those issues aren't mission-critical to the organization.

'So what data are you tracking?' 'We're tracking business data.' Which signals that numbers are more important to the organization than people. That, again, the what is more important than the how. Which is a problem. Yes, business metrics are indeed mission-critical because without them the organization would not have a competitive advantage. If it isn't disciplined around making sure its business is being run efficiently, it may not even continue to exist as an entity. But in operating a business, we also have to figure out how to manage people and performance. Which means measuring those things.

---

26 *Great Place To Work.* https://greatplacetowork.me/ (accessed March 27, 2025).

*In operating a business, we have to figure out how to
manage people and performance. Which means measuring
those things.*

We might turn Drucker's phrase around and say, 'What doesn't get measured, doesn't get managed.'

It is no good just having a short-term program—say, for one year—that captures this data. We need to commit to it in the long term. Otherwise, what we are signaling to our people is that we have only short-term interest in them. We aren't really looking at a sustainable solution to their problems because they aren't mission-critical.

To be fair, I don't think that this is a malicious approach. It may be that the organization doesn't have the internal capacity or expertise to collect the necessary data—in which case they might hire an external consultant and perhaps get caught out and have to ask (too late), 'Why are things the way they are?'.

Or it might simply be unconscious—a symptom of a lack of awareness of the importance of a people-centered leadership approach. And if the chief executive is focused only on business metrics, on the what and not the how, they will set the tone at the top and it will cascade through the organization until it permeates the workplace and a culture of ends justifying means develops as a result.

People and productivity

We have looked at the equation: Performance equals potential minus interference (see page 67). If an organization is to maximize performance, it must look at interference; it must ask, What is getting in the way of our performance? And it will see that a lot of that interference stems from conflict, a toxic workplace culture, a silo mentality, combative relationships between line manager and direct reports ... all the 'people' things we have been talking about.

If we can improve those things, there will be an exponential improvement in terms of overall productivity. Yet too many organizations put their head in the sand instead of confronting them and tackling them. Yes, it is difficult because we are talking about human emotions, but it isn't rocket science. Nor is it abstract art. It is measurable and it is manageable. If we can't locate the source of the interference, we probably aren't collecting the right data, so we need to start collecting a new set of data to help us understand what is getting in the way.

If we can't locate the source of the interference, we probably aren't collecting the right data.

Looking at it at the individual level, we may see that a person is high-performing (a 4 or a 5) but difficult to work with, which creates interference. But is it really that person who is responsible for the interference, or is it the people who are working with them? Is it *their* egos that are getting in the way? Do *they* need to manage their egos, set them to the side, zoom out and see the bigger picture?

As human beings we are prone to confirmation bias: We assume certain things to be the case and then filter what we see and hear in order to confirm that assumption. We do so to protect our self-esteem and minimize cognitive dissonance— or simply to make life easier. If someone has a reputation for being difficult to work with, we will tend to focus on things that confirm that reputation and fail to see the valuable contribution that they are making to the organization.

We should therefore be suspending judgment, taking a step back, and asking, 'Does this person add value to the enterprise?'.

If the answer is yes, then we need to work out what needs to happen in order for them to remain an important contributing factor to the entity's success. It may be that they need to be managed tightly, or held accountable, or mentored or coached around some of their behaviors that may be creating the difficulty to work with them ...

We must remember that as leaders we are fiduciaries. As such, we should be removing ourselves from the equation and thinking only in terms of making good decisions for the entity, for the enterprise. To think as a fiduciary requires us to be highly evolved human beings. It requires us to have respect, integrity, dignity, and empathy. These are the pillars of informed leadership that will lead to improved productivity, to improved performance.

Summary

As leaders we must give our direct reports the latitude to make their own (informed) decisions 'on the fly'. We must also 'allow' them to make mistakes and praise them for their good decisions rather than shaming them for their bad ones—though these must be assessed in a constructive way.

Making mistakes is part of the 'hardship' we must all endure in order to grow, so we should expose our direct reports to challenging experiences, even more than to developmental relationships, training, and study. This will improve their confidence and resourcefulness.

Instead of focusing solely on KPIs, which measure what has been achieved, we should also assess how those targets have (or haven't) been met. As well, we must establish a weighted system of shared KPIs for cross-functional collaboration.

Measuring business data is not enough; we must also track our people, including how they are performing and what 'interference' they may be experiencing (or causing). We should suspend judgment and avoid confirmation bias, asking what contribution individuals are making to the organization, and managing them accordingly.

10
Prosperity

Any misalignment of purpose or performance will result in a misalignment on prosperity, which requires a healthy and balanced relationship between leader and direct report.

In the opening chapter of this book, we talked about the social contract between employer and employee and how this has changed fundamentally in the last half-century; how the sense of 'employee loyalty' and 'job security' has been eroded and organizations are, on the one hand, finding it difficult to retain employees and, on the other, undervaluing them, which has led to a confused understanding of the employer–employee relationship and increasing levels of disengagement—in other words, to an absence of prosperity.

The recent Covid pandemic exacerbated this confusion by showing employees that remote work arrangements are possible while their employers were urging them to come back to the office. (Ironically, Zoom, the client utility business that allowed people to connect remotely, has itself mandated that the majority of its workforce should be office-based.) Whereas, once, it was 'acceptable' to just go to work, put your head down, and collect a paycheck at the end of the month, people are now asking for different things. Quality of life has taken priority, and talented people are choosing to take less if it allows them to work from home or to work remotely.

Many jobs can now be effectively done from home, or in a combination of remote and office work, which means that there is more optionality today. If we want to keep talented people in our organizations, we have to get the balance right.

If, at any point in the relationship, there is an imbalance, it is not good for either party. If organizations can't figure out a way to be highly desirable, with a mission that is so grand and purposeful that employees want to get behind it, they are going to struggle to attract people. Conversely, if they want to be gainfully employed, employees have to bring something to the table as well. There needs to be mutual respect and mutual benefits. Without them, the relationship will break down.

A two-way commitment

The relationship between employer and employee, between leader and direct report, will always be unbalanced in that the former has power over the latter, although, as we have seen, leaders must assume the responsibility that comes with that power. So what we are really talking about is not so much a balanced relationship as a balanced commitment to that relationship.

In this sense, prosperity is a two-way commitment. It has to work for both the employer and the employee, and there needs to be alignment. The employee must ask themselves what they can offer the organization in relation to its purpose and mission, while the organization must ask why a highly skilled individual who is highly desirable in the marketplace would want to work for it and what is going to anchor a win for organization and a win for that individual in coming to it.

To ensure that the organization is getting what it needs from its workforce and vice versa, we need a system of checks and balances. In his book *The 7 Habits of Highly Effective People*,[27] Stephen Covey talks about the 'P/PC balance', where P stands for production of desired results and PC for caring for what produces those results. Referring to the fable about the goose that laid the golden eggs, he warns that excessive focus on P frequently leads to unhappy employees, broken relationships, and poor health.

It can have even worse effects, as was shown by the Orange Telecom tragedy, in which a 'deep restructuring' of the business in the 2000s led to at least 18 suicides and 13 suicide attempts between April 2008 and June 2010. The finding of the French court in December 2019 that Orange—and in particular its then CEO Didier Lombard—were guilty of 'moral harassment' and that this was the cause of the deaths[28] was the first official sanction of irresponsible leadership practices, setting a precedent for other such cases to be brought against business leaders.

As such, we must therefore ask ourselves, 'What are our moral and ethical responsibilities toward our direct reports?

---

27 Free Press (1989).
28 Simon Carraud, 'French Telco Orange Found Guilty Over Workers' Suicides in Landmark Ruling', *Reuters*, December 21, 2019, https://www.reuters.com/article/business/french-telco-orange-found-guilty-over-workers-suicides-in-landmark-ruling-idUSKBN1YO15M/#:~:text=The%20court%20found%20Orange%20guilty,specialising%20in%20white%2Dcollar%20crime (accessed March 27, 2025).

What social contract with them are we committing to?'. If we ignore such questions, we could face dire consequences.

If we are serious about running an enterprise, it is no longer enough to make sure that shareholders are getting value for their money. We also need to ensure that our workforce is engaged and fulfilled, and that they are enjoying an appropriate quality of life. The fact that an employee is working for the organization doesn't necessarily mean that they must make concessions to its leadership team. There is an interdependence. The prosperity of the organization is not independent of but depends on the prosperity of its employees.

The prosperity of the organization is not independent of but depends on the prosperity of its employees.

A healthy 'bank balance'

In *The 7 Habits of Highly Effective People*, Stephen Covey also argues that leaders should think of the relationships they have with their team members as a bank account in which 'deposits' are made through positive and trusting interactions, which must (more than) balance any 'withdrawals' resulting from misunderstandings and broken commitments. Too many withdrawals and not enough deposits results in an 'overdraft'—in other words, a negative relationship. The important thing is that both sides must make regular deposits to maintain prosperity.

Another useful metaphor to keep in mind is that of having regular check-ups with your doctor or dentist. If you don't, and then one day need to visit them, you are likely to find that you are 'overdrawn on your account': that you have found out too late that you have a serious health problem.

These situations can be prevented by small actions, by making sure that you have line of sight on all the data you need: not just the business intelligence data that will help you to turn around your positioning in your marketplace versus your competitors or inform how you go to market with a new product or service, but also the personal data that will tell you what your organization's state of health is. And that data needs to be fresh enough for you to make informed decisions. If the data is out of date, those decisions could come too late to be effective.

Employee Value Proposition

To attract and retain employees, your organization needs a strong EVP. It needs to say, 'Listen, this is why you want to work for us. We offer you quality of life. We offer you good managers who care about what you do and give you the opportunity to grow.' They may not grow in a linear sense because there is only a finite number of senior roles that they can grow into, but you can offer them growth in terms of learning and development.

In Chapter 1 I said that talent development is one of the most difficult skills for leaders to acquire—and one of the most important. Now it should be clear why.

To attract and retain the best people, the organization should have a USP, a unique selling point beyond attractive salaries and bonuses. It might offer recreation rooms, free onsite nursery service, paid maternal/paternal leave, access to corporate discount cards, work policy that allows for a certain amount of work from home days in a month/quarter, catered food, whatever will make your organization more appealing than its competitors.

*To attract and retain the best people, the organization
should have a USP.*

This will also help it to achieve a high ranking in 'league tables' such as Great Place to Work, Trustindex,[29] or McKinsey's Organizational Health Index;[30] or acquire B Lab certification,[31] which will make you stand out even more in the marketplace and signal to potential employees that your organization is a good place to work.

Registering with these indices will also ensure that your organization is capturing the right data—people data, organizational health data—because they have proven data collection methodologies that correlate to overall organizational success.

Self-development

Search the internet for 'feelings about leadership' and you are likely to pick up a lot of negative commentary about leaders and how bad they are. As I have said before, it is not easy to be a leader, but—leaving aside those leaders who acquired their positions through nepotism or some other form of favoritism—it does require hard work and persistence to become one, which many people fail to acknowledge.

It is easy to criticize leaders and comment on how they can do a better job, but, to paraphrase American professor, social worker, and writer Brené Brown, if you are not in the arena getting your ass kicked, you are in no position to give them advice. Instead, they should be afforded respect for what they

29   See https://www.trustindex.io/, accessed March 27, 2025.
30   See https://www.mckinsey.com/solutions/orgsolutions/overview/
     organizational-health-index, accessed March 27, 2025.
31   See https://www.bcorporation.net/en-us/, accessed March 27, 2025.

have achieved and the pressure they have to handle on a day-to-day basis.

At the same time, however, leaders must be answerable to their direct reports. How often do I hear employees saying things like, 'My line manager has no idea. How can they not see ...?'. In most cases, they do not see because they aren't looking—or aren't looking in the right place. Because they aren't aware, because they don't have respect, integrity, dignity, and empathy. Because they aren't anti-fragile, bold, clear, and deliberate. They are leaders vis-à-vis the positions they hold, but they aren't informed leaders.

In order to have a prosperous relationship with your direct reports, you need to be committed to your own development—as a leader, as a person. You may not achieve mastery of informed leadership overnight, but you can acquire a strong command of it and put it into action in the areas of purpose, performance, and prosperity.

In order to have a prosperous relationship with your direct reports, you need to be committed to your own development.

Not only will this make you a more effective and confident leader, but the very fact that you are modeling informed leadership will also have a positive knock-on effect. Your direct reports will start to model their behavior on yours, their direct reports will follow their example, and so on down through the organization. You will be creating an operating system that can be replicated downstream at every level of leadership.

In doing so, you will be transforming and uplifting your workforce's ability to perform, which is the true meaning of optimization. You will be making your organization a Great Place to Work, attracting top talent, who will be happy to commit to work for you.

Summary

Misalignment of purpose or performance will result in a misalignment on prosperity, which is a healthy relationship ('social contract') between employer and employee. That relationship cannot be completely balanced, since employers have power over employees, but there needs to be a balanced commitment to it, and it must work for both parties: Each must get what they want out of the agreement.

From the leader's point of view, there must be a balance between production and producer, i.e. employee. If the former is prioritized and the latter ignored, there can be disastrous consequences—for which the leader can be held responsible in law.

We must acknowledge and respect the interdependence of employer and employed, and maintain a healthy 'bank balance' in terms of 'deposits' (of trusting interactions) and 'withdrawals' (broken commitments). Regular 'check-ups,' with fresh people data, can prevent serious organizational health problems.

Any organization needs a strong EVP, offering employees growth and other benefits that constitute its USP and give it a high ranking in business 'league tables.'

Entering the leadership 'arena' is risky and exposes you to criticism, so we must focus above all on our own development in terms of having respect, integrity, dignity, and empathy, in making ourselves anti-fragile, bold, clear, and deliberate—in sum, in becoming informed leaders.

Modeling informed leadership will have a cascading effect down through the business and make your organization a place where people want to work.

Conclusion

Life as a leader is tough—there are no two ways about it. It is easy to get lost and frustrated along the way and to become stuck, without being able to see the way out. It is a common problem in our increasingly VUCA world; it is understandable and, more importantly, human. But to *remain* stuck as a leader is simply not an option because there is a cost to inaction—and it is a high one.

Not only will your business suffer, and the people who are part of it, but you yourself will feel inadequate—both as a leader and as a person. When you look at yourself in the mirror and see your reflection looking back at you, you will always know that there was another way.

In this book I have outlined the four pillars of informed leadership: respect, integrity, dignity, and empathy; and shown how, together, they can help you to avoid the common leadership blind spots and find a way forward to achieve prosperity—both for your business and for yourself.

As the Stoics say, 'If you focus on you first and you get that right, the other things will fall into place.' If you haven't done your work, you won't be able to meet the challenges of leading others because you haven't solidified who *you* are and what your values are. You won't have a sense of right and wrong. You won't have an understanding of the qualities required of an effective leader. You won't have a navigational system that will enable you to orient yourself in difficult situations. You won't have a bigger purpose than just getting through the day—in which case, how can you possibly have the capacity to align yourself with your organization's purpose?

The four pillars will reflect your commitment to building yourself, to holding yourself to a higher standard, while also demonstrating your commitment to afford the same values to all those you come into contact with. A natural by-product of this commitment will be trust, which you will build by making regular deposits into your relationship bank account and maintaining a healthy balance.

Doing so will enable you to optimize the outcome you are looking for. It won't necessarily mean that you will succeed in every situation, but you will have laid a solid foundation to build on—a foundation that will withstand all the pressures and shocks that it is subjected to in your life as a leader.

You will encounter obstacles and interference, and these might impede your actions, but if you have built a solid foundation, your purpose, your intentions and your method of achieving that purpose and realizing those intentions will never be impeded and you will enjoy confidence in your leadership, knowing that it is founded on first principles, that it is truly informed leadership.

Acknowledgements

I'm deeply grateful to the early readers who generously gave their time, energy, and insight to this book. Many of you are trusted friends who are also leading businesses, and/or former clients who have become trusted friends—your thoughtful feedback sharpened the message, strengthened the clarity, and reminded me why this work matters. Thank you for believing in me and the vision of the book, and helping shape it into something worthy of leaders' time.

Works Cited

Chapter 1

Armstrong, Martin. "Why People are Quitting Their Jobs." *Statistica*. July 25, 2022, https://www.statista.com/chart/27830/reasons-for-quitting-previous-job (accessed March 25, 2025).

Harter, Jim. "U.S. Engagement Hits 11-Year Low." *Gallup Workplace*. April 10, 2024, https://www.gallup.com/workplace/643286/engagement-hits-11-year-low.aspx#:~:text=Last%20year%2C%20Gallup%20found%20U.S.%20employees%20were%20increasingly,to%20feel%20someone%20at%20work%20cares%20about%20them (accessed March 25, 2025).

Korn Ferry. *Global Competency Framework*. https://store.kornferry.com/en/product/5d7bc4a3-c28a-47eb-b8d1-47bc293e65ff (accessed March 25, 2025).

Korn Ferry. *Korn Ferry Leadership Architect™ Technical Manual*. https://www.scribd.com/document/354060738/KFLA-Technical-Manual (accessed Mar. 25, 2025).

Parker, Kim and Horowitz, Juliana. "Majority of Workers Who Quit a Job in 2021 Cite Low Pay, No Opportunities for Advancement, Feeling Disrespected." *Pew Research Center.* March 9, 2022, https://www.pewresearch.org/short-reads/2022/03/09/majority-of-workers-who-quit-a-job-in-2021-cite-low-pay-no-opportunities-for-advancement-feeling-disrespected/#:~:text=A%20new%20Pew%20Research%20Center%20survey%20finds%20that,reasons%20why%20Americans%20quit%20their%20jobs%20last%20year (accessed March 25, 2025).

Pencavel, John. *Diminishing Returns at Work: The Consequence of Long Working Hours.* Oxford University Press, 2018.

Reid, Erin. "Why Some Men Pretend to Work 80-Hour Weeks." *Harvard Business Review.* April 29, 2015, https://hbr.org/2015/04/why-some-men-pretend-to-work-80-hour-weeks (accessed March 25, 2025).

Russell Reynolds. *Leadership Confidence Index.* https://www.russellreynolds.com/en/insights/reports-surveys/leadership-confidence-index (accessed March 25, 2025).

Tuckman, Bruce. "Developmental Sequence in Small Groups." *Psychological Bulletin* 63, no. 6 (1965): 384–399. https://psycnet.apa.org/doiLanding?doi=10.1037%2Fh0022100

Chapter 2

Mill, J. S. *On Liberty.* Bobbs-Merrill, 1859.

Pfeffer, Jeffrey. Leadership BS: Fixing Workplaces and Careers One Truth at a Time. HarperBusiness, 2015.

Smith, Morgan. "71% of CEOs in the U.S. say they have imposter syndrome: 'It's a crisis of confidence'." *CNBC Make It*. June 7, 2024, https://www.cnbc.com/2024/06/07/71percent-of-ceos-in-the-us-say-they-have-imposter-syndrome-says-new-report.html (accessed March 25, 2025).

Chapter 3
Christensen, Clayton. *How Will You Measure Your Life?* Thorsons, 2019.

Green, Charles, Galford, Robert, and Maister, David. *The Trusted Adviser.* Simon and Schuster, 2001.

Patel, Alok and Plowman, Stephanie. "The Increasing Importance of a Best Friend at Work." *Gallup Workplace.* August 17, 2022, https://www.gallup.com/workplace/397058/increasing-importance-best-friend-work.aspx#:~:text=Gallup%20data%20indicate%20that%20having,safety%2C%20inventory%20control%20and%20retention (accessed March 27, 2025).

Chapter 4
Oxford English Dictionary Online, s.v. "Integrity", accessed March 27, 2025, www.oed.com/dictionary/integrity_n?tl=true

Chapter 5
Campbell, Joseph. *The Hero's Journey.* 3rd ed. New World Library, 2014.

Gallwey, Timothy. *The Inner Game®.* https://theinnergame.com (accessed March 27, 2025).

Chapter 6

Cambridge Dictionary Online, s.v. "Empathy", accessed March 27, 2025, https://dictionary.cambridge.org/dictionary/english/empathy

Holiday, Ryan. *The Obstacle is the Way*. Profile Books, 2015.

Chapter 7

Ericsson, Anders and Pool, Robert. *Peak: Secrets from the New Science of Expertise*. Houghton Mifflin Harcourt, 2016.

Klass, Brian. Corruptible: Who Gets Power and How It Changes Us. John Murray, 2022.

Taleb, Nassim. Antifragile: Things that Gain from Disorder. Penguin, 2013.

Chapter 8

Argyris, Chris. *Integrating the Individual and the Organization*. John Wiley and Sons, Inc., 1964.

Argyris, Chris. *On Organizational Learning*. Blackwell Publishers, 1999.

Argyris, Chris. *Organizational Traps: Leadership, Culture, Organizational Design*. Oxford, 2010.

Fraser, David. "What's the Difference Between Espoused Theories and Theories in Use?" *Dr David Fraser*, March 20, 2015, https://drdavidfraser.com/2015/03/20/whats-the-difference-between-espoused-theories-and-theories-in-use/ (accessed March 27, 2025).

Chapter 9

Center for Creative Leadership, https://www.ccl.org/ (accessed March 27, 2025).

Great Place To Work, https://greatplacetowork.me/ (accessed March 27, 2025).

Chapter 10

B Lab. *B Lab Global Site*. https://www.bcorporation.net/en-us/ (accessed March 27, 2025).

Carraud, Simon. "French Telco Orange Found Guilty Over Workers' Suicides in Landmark Ruling." *Reuters*, December 21, 2019. https://www.reuters.com/article/business/french-telco-orange-found-guilty-over-workers-suicides-in-landmark-ruling-idUSKBN1YO15M/#:~:text=The%20court%20found%20Orange%20guilty,specialising%20in%20white%2Dcollar%20crime (accessed March 27, 2025).

Covey, Stephen. *The 7 Habits of Highly Effective People*. Free Press, 1989.

McKinsey. *Trust Index*. https://www.trustindex.io (accessed March 27, 2025).

McKinsey. *Organizational Health Index*. https://www.mckinsey.com/solutions/orgsolutions/overview/organizational-health-index (accessed March 27, 2025).

The Author

David Ribott, Ed.D. (ABD), MCC

Founder of Ribott Partners | Board & Leadership Advisor |
CEO Coach | Author & Speaker

From the South Bronx to the boardrooms of the Middle East, David Ribott has forged a path as a trusted advisor to purpose-driven CEOs and boards who aim to unlock long-term value, preserve legacy, and lead with integrity. With over two decades of experience guiding leadership teams across EMEA and APAC, David blends behavioral insight, governance expertise, and performance coaching into a unique framework that has redefined executive leadership for the modern age.

David founded Ribott Partners in 2015 to advise the boards and management teams of multinational corporations, family enterprises, and government institutions on leadership development, assessment and succession planning, and complex organizational transformation. His achievements include guiding more than a dozen first-time CEOs through the onboarding process to transition successfully into their new roles as heads of their enterprises, helping CXOs at ACWA

Power lead the transition from pre-IPO to IPO stage to become one of the largest listings in MENA, providing M&A executive assessment support of CXO leaders for two of the largest bank mergers in MENA, and partnering with family businesses to ensure succession sustainability between the generations and fortify their legacy ambitions.

An athlete turned leadership strategist, David's early discipline in American football formed the foundation of his executive coaching program where he applies his signature *Corporate Athlete Approach* to coach CEOs like elite athletes for peak performance, resilience, and clarity under pressure. David has worked with organizations like Majid Al Futtaim, Boehringer Ingelheim, and Emirates Global Aluminum to help develop senior leaders to be able to manage the pace of change and complexity while having the ability to drive results through others. He worked closely with them to create a culture of high performance within their teams and build capability in their organizations.

When he's not in the boardroom or coaching C-suite leaders, David is contributing to global business forums as both a facilitator and speaker, advocating for governance innovation, and mentoring leaders from family businesses, aviation, financial services, government, pharma, and construction who will shape tomorrow's world.

David is an accredited board director and mediator, and a Master Certified Coach. David holds a Master's degree in Sociolinguistics and is also a certified strengths coach and assessor of leadership potential.

He was born in Spanish Harlem, raised in the South Bronx, and has been living in Abu Dhabi for the past 17 years. David's favorite person is his 10-year-old son, Leo.

www.ingramcontent.com/pod-product-compliance
Lightning Source LLC
Chambersburg PA
CBHW071645210326
41597CB00017B/2124